MW01146169

# A RAISIN IN THE SUN

THE GREENHAVEN PRESS
*Literary Companion*
TO AMERICAN LITERATURE

# A RAISIN IN THE SUN

Lawrence Kappel, *Book Editor*

David L. Bender, *Publisher*
Bruno Leone, *Executive Editor*
Bonnie Szumski, *Series Editor*

Greenhaven Press, Inc., San Diego, CA

Every effort has been made to trace the owners of copy-righted material. The articles in this volume may have been edited for content, length, and/or reading level. The titles have been changed to enhance the editorial purpose. Those interested in locating the original source will find the complete citation on the first page of each article.

Library of Congress Cataloging-in-Publication Data

Readings on A raisin in the sun / Lawrence Kappel, book editor.
        p.      cm. — (The Greenhaven Press literary companion to American literature)
    Includes bibliographical references and index.
    ISBN 0-7377-0368-7 (lib. bdg. : alk. paper). —
ISBN 0-7377-0367-9 (pbk. : alk. paper)
    1. Hansberry, Lorraine, 1930–1965. Raisin in the sun.
2. Domestic drama, American—History and criticism.
3. Afro-American families in literature. 4. Afro-Americans in literature. I. Kappel, Lawrence. II. Series.

PS3515.A515 R3385    2001
812'.54—dc21                                        99-086356

Cover photo: Bettmann/CORBIS

Copyright © 2001 by Greenhaven Press, Inc.
PO Box 289009
San Diego, CA 92198-9009
Printed in the U.S.A.

*"Vulgarity, blind conformity and mass lethargy need not triumph in the land of Lincoln and Frederick Douglass and Walt Whitman and Mark Twain. There is simply no reason why dreams should dry up like raisins or prunes or anything else in America."*

—*Lorraine Hansberry*
To Be Young, Gifted, and Black

# CONTENTS

## Chapter 1: An African American Play

## Chapter 2: The Female Aspect of the Play

breakdown of the family or view it as an obstacle to personal fulfillment, *Raisin* celebrates the family as a vital context for individual growth.

# Chapter 5: The Play in Various Forms

successful adaptation was written by Hansberry's former husband and collaborator, Robert Nemiroff. Some critics declare the musical superior to the original play.

## 4. The 1989 Video Revival and the Restored Scenes

*Raisin* received renewed attention in the late 1980s when a new production of the play starring Danny Glover was produced by the American Playhouse for the Public Broadcasting Service. Nemiroff discusses scenes cut from the 1959 play and looks back at *Raisin* after almost thirty years.

# FOREWORD

*"'Tis the good reader that
makes the good book."*

Ralph Waldo Emerson

The story's bare facts are simple: The captain, an old and
scarred seafarer, walks with a peg leg made of whale ivory.
He relentlessly drives his crew to hunt the world's oceans for
the great white whale that crippled him. After a long search,
the ship encounters the whale and a fierce battle ensues. Finally the captain drives his harpoon into the whale, but the
harpoon line catches the captain about the neck and drags
him to his death.

A simple story, a straightforward plot—yet, since the 1851
publication of Herman Melville's *Moby-Dick*, readers and
critics have found many meanings in the struggle between
Captain Ahab and the whale. To some, the novel is a cau-
tionary tale that depicts how Ahab's obsession with revenge
leads to his insanity and death. Others believe that the whale
represents the unknowable secrets of the universe and that
Ahab is a tragic hero who dares to challenge fate by attempt-
ing to discover this knowledge. Perhaps Melville intended
Ahab as a criticism of Americans' tendency to become involved in well-intentioned but irrational causes. Or did Melville model Ahab after himself, letting his fictional character
express his anger at what he perceived as a cruel and distant
god?

Although literary critics disagree over the meaning of
*Moby-Dick*, readers do not need to choose one particular interpretation in order to gain an understanding of Melville's

novel. Instead, by examining various analyses, they can gain numerous insights into the issues that lie under the surface of the basic plot. Studying the writings of literary critics can also aid readers in making their own assessments of *Moby-Dick* and other literary works and in developing analytical thinking skills.

The Greenhaven Literary Companion Series was created with these goals in mind. Designed for young adults, this unique anthology series provides an engaging and comprehensive introduction to literary analysis and criticism. The essays included in the Literary Companion Series are chosen for their accessibility to a young adult audience and are expertly edited in consideration of both the reading and comprehension levels of this audience. In addition, each essay is introduced by a concise summation that presents the contributing writer's main themes and insights. Every anthology in the Literary Companion Series contains a varied selection of critical essays that cover a wide time span and express diverse views. Wherever possible, primary sources are represented through excerpts from authors' notebooks, letters, and journals and through contemporary criticism.

Each title in the Literary Companion Series pays careful consideration to the historical context of the particular author or literary work. In-depth biographies and detailed chronologies reveal important aspects of authors' lives and emphasize the historical events and social milieu that influenced their writings. To facilitate further research, every anthology includes primary and secondary source bibliographies of articles and/or books selected for their suitability for young adults. These engaging features make the Greenhaven Literary Companion series ideal for introducing students to literary analysis in the classroom or as a library resource for young adults researching the world's great authors and literature.

Exceptional in its focus on young adults, the Greenhaven Literary Companion Series strives to present literary criticism in a compelling and accessible format. Every title in the series is intended to spark readers' interest in leading American and world authors, to help them broaden their understanding of literature, and to encourage them to formulate their own analyses of the literary works that they read. It is the editors' hope that young adult readers will find these anthologies to be true companions in their study of literature.

# INTRODUCTION

In 1959, when the play *A Raisin in the Sun* opened on Broadway starring Sidney Poitier and Claudia McNeil, the civil rights movement of the 1960s was barely underway. Martin Luther King Jr. would not give his "I Have a Dream" speech for another four years, and the Student Nonviolent Coordinating Committee (SNCC) would not even exist for another year. Lorraine Hansberry's play was a harbinger of things to come in its depiction of the African American Younger family after several generations trying to seize full access to the American dream—whether in the form of Walter's business venture, Beneatha's unlimited career choice, or the best possible home of their own for the whole family, even if it happens to be in a previously all-white neighborhood. Five years later, when SNCC would become world famous as the spearhead of the civil rights movement, the group would choose Hansberry as the most appropriate author to write the text for its official book of photographs, *The Movement: Documentary of a Struggle for Equality.*

Beyond the demand for equality and integration, *Raisin* also predicts the focus on ethnic pride and honoring one's pre-American cultural roots. In the 1970s this emphasis would follow the civil rights movement as a significant social trend. The intelligent and sophisticated Nigerian character Joseph Asagai is a credible and attractive alternative to what had been the predominant depiction in American culture of black Africans as primitives, as in the Tarzan films of the 1930s and 1940s. The wise Asagai is Hansberry's exemplar of selfless idealism that transcends despair. Beneatha's enthusiasm for her African heritage provides references throughout the play to genuine African history and culture.

This remarkably prophetic play also foresees the women's movement in Beneatha's being a prototype of the newly empowered woman of the 1970s. She makes career choices for herself traditionally reserved for men. Matriarch Lena represents the heroic but more traditionally family-oriented woman admired in the neoconservative 1980s. And Ruth, somewhere between Beneatha and Lena, illustrates the dilemma of being wife, mother, and worker as well, without time for herself. *Raisin* thus provides a rich context for consideration of American womanhood and its recent evolution. Likewise, *Raisin*'s concern with the dignity of manhood and the role of provider in an oppressive society is expressed through the legacy that Walter receives from his father, the same one he passes on to his own son. In this, the play offers a significant preview of the men's movement of the 1980s and 1990s as well.

With its previews of the civil rights, ethnic pride, feminist, and men's movements, *Raisin* was a midcentury crystal ball of the social trends that would express the democratic process in the United States in the second half of the twentieth century.

Since the 1990s, especially after the widely acclaimed 1989 American Playhouse/PBS video version starring Danny Glover and Esther Rolle, *A Raisin in the Sun* has been increasingly recognized by critics as even more than a skillfully constructed and clairvoyant social commentary. In its emotional, psychological, and philosophical depth, *Raisin* is a modern American classic, a great family drama that belongs in the company of Eugene O'Neill's *Long Day's Journey into Night*, Arthur Miller's *Death of a Salesman*, and Tennessee Williams's *The Glass Menagerie*. Like them, it transcends race, ethnicity, and gender, ultimately being universal in its significance.

## VERSIONS OF *RAISIN*

On its way to becoming a standard text of American culture, *Raisin* went through several important incarnations. Running for 530 performances, the original 1959 Broadway production won the New York Drama Critics' Circle Award for best play of the year, beating plays by O'Neill and Williams, making Hansberry the first African American, only the fifth woman, and, at age twenty-nine, the youngest playwright to win the prestigious award.

A successful film version followed in 1961 featuring Sidney Poitier, Claudia McNeil, and the original Broadway cast, and it won a special award from the international Cannes Film Festival. The screenplay was written by Hansberry herself, her earlier screenplay having been rejected by the producers as too controversial. This originally rejected screenplay was published for the first time in 1992.

Twelve years after the film, *Raisin* received new life yet again as a hit Broadway musical in 1973. This version was adapted and produced by Hansberry's former husband, collaborator, and literary executor, Robert Nemiroff. The musical won the Tony Award as best musical that season and ran for 847 performances, even longer than the original play. By this time, the original play had been performed thousands of times across the United States and had been translated into thirty languages and produced worldwide. But it was the "Twenty-Fifth Anniversary Revival"—first produced at the Roundabout Theatre in New York in 1986 and later televised in 1989 starring Danny Glover and Esther Rolle—that focused attention on *Raisin*'s status as a classic.

The critical essays selected for this Greenhaven Literary Companion to Lorraine Hansberry's *A Raisin in the Sun* include specific discussions of the original 1959 production, the 1961 film, the 1973 musical, the 1989 video, and the unfilmed screenplay (written in 1961 but published more than three decades later, in 1992). In addition, they include studies of each of the major characters, and they represent various perspectives: African American, female, and universal. Each of the essays is introduced by a guide to its key points, which are further identified within the essays through subheadings. As a further aid to understanding, inserts within selected essays illuminate important ideas and add supplemental information. An annotated table of contents offers brief previews of the individual essays as well.

Also in this Greenhaven Literary Companion are a detailed biographical introduction and an overview of the play's plot and characters for convenient reference. A chronology of key dates in Hansberry's life and career provides historical context. Further reading on Hansberry and *Raisin* is indicated, and research is facilitated by a bibliography that avoids excessively scholarly and theoretical material. These tools and the essays themselves provide the basis of an enhanced and enriched reading of *A Raisin in the Sun*.

# LORRAINE HANSBERRY: MANY ROLES IN A LIFE AND CAREER TOO BRIEF

Lorraine Hansberry's life was appropriately dramatic for a playwright. When she died of cancer at age thirty-four, she was widely mourned not only because of her fame and youth but also because of the loss of the work she might have produced had she lived even a few years longer. But tragic victim was not her first role.

Hansberry had already played five other dramatic parts in her adult life, beginning with her experience as a political activist. She spent her late teens and early twenties attending demonstrations, giving speeches, traveling, and writing on behalf of radical causes, which led to her passport being revoked by the U.S. government. She then embraced a second role as a full-time writer, working solo on three plays simultaneously for the next several years.

A third part Hansberry played—that of celebrity—was given to her by others and was based on the sudden and overwhelming success of *A Raisin in the Sun* on Broadway in 1959. Hansberry was cast in the familiar role in American culture of the "overnight sensation" who goes from obscurity to massive public acclaim seemingly in a single stroke. After years of struggle, Hansberry first welcomed the attention and praise, but she soon discovered that her fame distracted and insulated her, making it harder for her to write.

It soon became clear that beyond the superficial celebrity role was a more significant fourth role as a cultural pioneer and prophet. *Raisin* inspired a new and powerful African American theater movement, and Hansberry was visionary in her forecast of the civil rights, women's, and ethnic pride movements that would transform American life in the decades following her play.

Celebrity also led to a decidedly unwelcome fifth role—as a target of political criticism. She was chided for having come

15

from a wealthy family, for not being radical enough, and for favoring integration over black power. By the time she was given her sixth and final role by fate, as victim in her struggle with cancer, Hansberry was a controversial figure, and the political criticism would continue for years after her death in 1965.

## POSTHUMOUS ROLES

Remarkably, the evolution of Hansberry's roles continued after she died. In 1969 her former husband and collaborator, Robert Nemiroff, constructed from her writings an "autobiography" entitled *To Be Young, Gifted, and Black.* The title was taken from a speech Hansberry had given to winners of a United Negro College Fund writing contest. It was very successful as an off-Broadway play, a national touring company, a book, and a pop song by Nina Simone. Thus, Hansberry's role as a cultural pioneer was renewed when she was cast as a symbolic mentor to and icon of a new generation of talented and committed minority American artists and writers.

The final part that Hansberry has come to play has taken the more than forty years since the original production of *Raisin* to be fully recognized. It is that of a classic American dramatist whose work is timeless and universal, appreciated and valued by successive generations of people all over the world.

What makes Hansberry's life and career so rich and complex is not only that she played so many different roles in so short a time, but that they were cumulative. Activist, writer, cultural pioneer, celebrity, political target—when she took on a new role, she did not abandon her old ones but continued to function in them, playing these roles not only successively but also simultaneously.

## A VERY HUMAN PERSON

To examine these roles is a meaningful way to account for Hansberry's life and career, but in addition to the parts Hansberry played, she was first of all a very human person:

> There are those who think me the liveliest of types: a chattering, guitar-playing, slow-drag dancing, guzzling figure of renaissance well-being. And, still, there are the others, those latter-day images of the children of my youth who found me curious then—and still do. A serious odd-talking kid who could neither jump double dutch nor understand their games, but who—classically—envied them.[1]

She had the insight and self-knowledge to see herself as paradoxically both extroverted and introverted, depending on whose company she was in. And because she admired her classmates from poor families, she was most self-conscious around them. Such a self-description reminds us that beyond her activities and accomplishments was a very real and complex person.

The writer James Baldwin captured Hansberry's personality as a friend in a tribute that he called "Sweet Lorraine." It is an eloquent suggestion of her character:

> We walked and talked and laughed and drank together . . . sometimes seeming for anyone who didn't know us to be having a knockdown, drag-out battle. We spent a lot of time arguing about history and tremendously related subjects in her . . . flat. And often, just when I was certain that she was about to throw me out, as being altogether too rowdy a type, she would stand up, her hands on her hips . . . and pick up my empty glass as though she intended to throw it at me. Then she would walk into the kitchen, saying, with a haughty toss of her head, "Really, Jimmy. You ain't *right*, child!" With which stern put-down, she would hand me another drink and launch into a brilliant analysis of just why I wasn't "right." I would often stagger down her stairs as the sun came up, usually in the middle of a paragraph and always in the middle of a laugh. That marvelous laugh. That marvelous face. I loved her, she was my sister and my comrade.[2]

Baldwin's writing skill evokes Hansberry as an individual and thereby gives meaning to his feeling of loss. It also suggests the vitality, the humor, and the humanity that enabled her to play so many significant roles in her short life.

## FROM SLAVERY TO BANKING AND REAL ESTATE

Hansberry's maternal grandparents were both born into slavery in Tennessee. When her grandfather Perry was a little boy, he ran away from his master and hid in the hills, where his mother would sneak him food by moonlight. The runaway slave boy later became a minister, eventually rising to the level of bishop in his church. He sent his daughter, Nannie Perry (Hansberry's mother), to college to be a teacher before World War I, when it was remarkable for any woman, black or white, to go on to higher education.

Years later, Nannie took her own children, including seven-year-old Lorraine, back to Tennessee to meet their grandmother, then an octogenarian in the final year of her life. This was the occasion of Lorraine's first learning about the concept of slavery and the facts of African American history. Meeting her own elderly grandmother, who had actually been a slave, and hearing the story of her grandfather's escape made a deep impression on her and inspired her to write a play about slavery for television many years later called *The Drinking Gourd*. "She was born in slavery and had memories of it and they didn't sound anything like *Gone with the Wind*,"[3] Hansberry said of her grandmother.

Lorraine's father, Carl Augustus Hansberry, was the well-educated son of respected schoolteachers in the tiny hamlet of Gloster, Mississippi. As a young man, he migrated north to Chicago and became an accountant for Binga National Bank, the city's first African American bank. Soon the ambitious and enterprising Hansberry founded a bank of his own, the Lake Street Bank, where he eventually met Nannie, who was employed there as a teller.

Hansberry's parents courted, married, settled down on the South Side of Chicago, and started a family. Lorraine, born in 1930, was the baby, with two brothers and a sister who were twelve, ten, and seven years older than she. Growing up, Lorraine often felt like an only child. She was isolated by her separateness from her older siblings, and she learned to entertain herself, especially by reading. She very much admired her father as a fearless hero, "a man who always seemed to be doing something brilliant and/or unusual to such an extent that to be doing something brilliant and/or unusual was the way I assumed fathers behaved."[4]

The Hansberrys succeeded not only in banking but also, and especially, in real estate. They remained involved in the real estate business throughout the 1920s and even during the Great Depression of the 1930s. As a prosperous upper-middle-class family, they were thought of by others as rich and therefore privileged. The Hansberry family, however, believed deeply in democratic ideals, and Mr. Hansberry ran for U.S. Congress as a Republican. Lorraine was "born into material comfort, yet baptized in social responsibility,"[5] wrote Jean Carey Bond, an editor of *Freedomways* magazine. For example, although he could afford it, Mr. Hansberry chose not to send his children to private schools because he believed in public education as a matter of democratic principle. As a result, Lorraine ironically received an inferior education in the segregated public schools of Chicago and had problems with basic arithmetic all of her life.

## A White Fur Coat and a Howling Mob

When Lorraine was five, she received a white fur coat for Christmas; and when she wore it to school, her resentful poor classmates threw ink on the coat and beat her up. As an adult, she looked back on this experience as a turning point: "Ever since then [I] had been antagonistic to the symbols of affluence. In fact, after that day [I] had chosen [my] friends with intense fascination from among—[my] assailants."[6] Ironically, in befriending these classmates, Lorraine was already fulfilling her family's legacy of social responsibility and setting her own course as an activist. The role of snooty rich kid was one she refused.

She was drawn to her less well-off friends not by pity but rather by envy of their access to adult experiences from which her wealthy background protected her. Above all, she envied their toughness and willingness to fight. Similarly, she was aware that her father was a man of principle who was willing to fight for what he believed in. Those qualities of Mr. Hansberry had a dramatic effect on the whole family in 1938, when Lorraine was eight years old.

At that time her father bought a house in an all-white neighborhood on the South Side, near the University of Chicago, just as the Younger family does in A *Raisin in the Sun.* And the neighborhood did not welcome the Hansberrys, just as the white neighborhood does not welcome the Youngers in *Raisin.* Lorraine described the experience many years later:

> My father was typical of a generation of Negroes who believed that the "American way" could successfully be made to work to democratize the United States. Thus . . . he spent a small personal fortune, his considerable talents, and many years of his life fighting, in association with NAACP [National Association for the Advancement of Colored People] attorneys, Chicago's "restrictive covenants" in one of this nation's ugliest ghettoes.
>
> That fight also required that our family occupy the disputed property in a hellishly hostile "white neighborhood" in which, literally, howling mobs surrounded our house. One of their missiles almost took the life of the then eight-year-old signer of this letter. My memories . . . include being spat at, cursed and pummeled in the daily trek to and from school. And I also remember my desperate and courageous mother, patrolling our house all night with a loaded German luger [pistol], doggedly guarding her four children, while my father fought the respectable part of the battle in the Washington court.[7]

Lorraine thus came to admire her mother's courage as much as her father's, and when she wrote *Raisin* twenty years later she created a hero in the mother character, Lena, and dedicated the play "to Mama: *in gratitude for the dream.*" The first draft of *A Raisin in the Sun* would end with the Younger family sitting in their darkened new house awaiting violence from their white neighbors, as Lorraine recalled in memories. In 1940 Mr. Hansberry finally won his case in a landmark decision of the U.S. Supreme Court, *Hansberry v. Lee,* further enhancing his reputation as a public-spirited man and a hero in the black community.

## DISTINGUISHED GUESTS

The Hansberry household thus became a focal point of African American life in Chicago, where among their visitors were prominent black celebrities, leaders, artists, and intellectuals. The guests included figures such as heavyweight boxing champion Joe Louis and Olympic gold medalist Jesse Owens, heroes not only to blacks but also to all of America following their dramatic victories over Aryan and German opponents who represented Adolf Hitler's "master race." Another guest was the great American composer Duke Ellington, a suave and sophisticated international celebrity.

The eminent sociology professor W.E.B. Du Bois was yet another frequent guest. A founder and guiding spirit of the NAACP, which had sponsored Mr. Hansberry's court battle, Du Bois had fought for and exemplified since the turn of the century black intellectual achievement at the highest level and the refusal to accept second-class citizenship. In 1940 Du Bois was more than seventy years old, still intellectually active and vigorous, and growing ever more doubtful that black people of African descent would ever be truly recognized as full-fledged Americans.

Other honored guests at the Hansberry home included the brilliant singing and acting star Paul Robeson, who had been an all-American college athlete and an attorney with an Ivy League law degree. After World War II Robeson would become a political activist, publishing a radical monthly magazine where Lorraine would work when she later became an activist herself. Poet Langston Hughes, whose "Montage of a Dream Deferred" was the source of the title *A Raisin in the Sun,* also visited their home. Finally, there was Lorraine's uncle, Professor Leo Hansberry of Howard University, a pioneer scholar of African studies whose research celebrated the achievements of ancient African civilizations. His reputation was such that leaders of the emerging democratic states in Africa would come to Howard to study African history under him, and a college at the University of Nigeria would be named after him in 1963.

This, then, is the milieu in which Lorraine grew up. The glamour of her parents' household is summed up by Hansberry expert Steven R. Carter: "The family living room was a mecca of conviviality and discussion for makers and shakers, doers and dreamers from all walks of black life and of all shades of opinion."[8]

## GROWTH AND LOSS

By the time she graduated from elementary school, Lorraine's awareness of her African heritage and her knowledge of history showed in her official choice of heroes in her autograph book: Toussaint-Louverture, the Haitian slave who led the revolution that overthrew French control of his Caribbean nation in the 1790s, and Hannibal, the ancient Carthaginian general whose North African armies defeated Rome in the Second Punic War during the third century B.C.

Lorraine's professional ambitions were focused on law and commercial art, and she was succeeding in school despite the inadequacies of her substandard math background. As a high school freshman she wrote a short story about football that won a school writing contest and established her talent, despite the fact that her entire knowledge of football had been acquired during a brief chat with one of her sister Mamie's dates.

For Mr. Hansberry, however, the World War II years following his Supreme Court victory were disappointing and frustrating. Racism seemed as bad as ever, and the segregated state of the U.S. Army, experienced firsthand by his son Carl Jr., made a mockery of his "victory" over segregated housing. Despairing over his inability to achieve equality in the United States despite all of his exhausting efforts, he bought a house in Mexico and planned to relocate his family there. But then this extraordinarily capable man died prematurely at age fifty-one "of a cerebral hemorrhage, supposedly," said Lorraine, "but American racism helped kill him."[9]

At the time of her father's death, Lorraine was fifteen, still young enough to idolize him yet old enough to understand some of his feeling of defeat. Like the Younger family in *A Raisin in the Sun,* the Hansberrys recognized a turning point and an occasion for self-definition when they considered the meaning of their father's life and death as their legacy. Many years later Lorraine would say, "I'm afraid I have to agree with Daddy's assessment of this country, but I don't agree with the leaving part."[10] Her father's death showed how powerful an enemy racism could be and strengthened her resolve to fight it.

### COLLEGE YEARS

Academic success continued as Hansberry became president of the high school debating society. She then went on in 1948 to the University of Wisconsin at Madison, where she was the first African American to live in her dormitory. In college she pursued her already-defined interest in politics and public affairs by taking history and philosophy courses and by becoming chairman of the radical Young Progressives of America. In the presidential election of 1948, when most voters were deciding between Republican Thomas Dewey and Democrat Harry Truman, Hansberry worked for the Progressive candidate Henry Wallace. At the same time, she pursued her interest in art by taking studio courses. Having been exposed to plays such as Shakespeare's *Othello* (starring family friend Paul Robeson) and *The Tempest* in high school, she took courses in literature and in stage set design as well.

But perhaps Hansberry's most important college experience was seeing a performance of Sean O'Casey's play *Juno and the Paycock*. An old Irish mother's cry of pain for her dead son in the play awoke something in the African American teenager in the audience:

> The woman's voice, the howl, the shriek of misery fitted to a wail of poetry that consumed all my senses and all my awareness of human pain, endurance and the futility of it. . . . And the wail rose and hummed through the tenement, through Dublin, through Ireland itself and then mingled with seas and became something borne of the Irish that was all of us. . . .
>
> I was seventeen and I did not think then of *writing* the melody as *I* knew it—in a different key; but I believe it entered my consciousness and stayed there.[11]

The inspiration of O'Casey's being most universal when he is being most Irish is the key to Hansberry's universality as a playwright—she is also most universal when she embraces and expresses her specific identity as a black woman. She pursued her new interest in modern international drama by reading and seeing plays by two great Scandinavian pioneers of modern drama, Norwegian Henrik Ibsen and Swede August Strindberg. According to Hansberry, "The theatre came into my life like *k-pow!*"[12]

Hansberry's college experiences were not all positive, however. She had problems in math and science, and she had little patience with courses that did not seem relevant to her, such as geology. The routine of going to class and taking notes seemed deadening, taking tests and getting grades childish. She disliked the idea of an ivory tower above and removed from real life. She was not in flight from the real world; she was hungry for it. Like Beneatha in *A Raisin in the Sun*, she was on a quest for her identity, and if that necessitated leaving college, so be it.

## DROPPING OUT

As with many of the 1960s generation, on whom Hansberry would have a great influence, dropping out of school was not seen as a gesture of despair, confusion, or defeat but as a positive step in personal growth and self-discovery. Her alienation from school was crystallized in a campus visit by the maverick American architect Frank Lloyd Wright: "He attacked almost everything. . . . He attacked babbitry [provincialism] and the nature of education saying that we put in so many fine plums and get out so many fine prunes. I left the University shortly after to pursue an education of another kind."[15]

At the age of twenty, after two years at the university and without a degree, Hansberry moved to New York City, ready to play the roles adult life would offer her. When she arrived in the fall of 1950, she found a place to live on the Lower East Side with three roommates, and she continued "finding herself" by enrolling in courses in jewelry making, photography, and short-story writing. She also attended political meetings and wrote articles for *Young Progressives* magazine. For a while she felt scattered, going in too many directions at once.

## ACTIVIST: *"THE* JOURNAL OF NEGRO LIBERATION"

After a couple of months, Hansberry found work writing for *Freedom,* a radical black monthly political magazine, and this became her focus. In a letter to a friend, she said, "I work for the new Negro paper, FREEDOM, which in its time in history ought to be *the* journal of Negro liberation. . . . In fact, it will be."[14] She moved to Harlem, where the magazine was based, and for the next two years political activism became for her a vocation, a commitment, and a way of life.

Still twenty, she was the youngest staff member at *Freedom* when she was hired, but in less than a year she was promoted to associate editor. She investigated and reported on discrimination, police brutality, and political trials in New

York, and she traveled to cover stories and attend political events in Mississippi; Washington, D.C.; and South America. She also marched in demonstrations and gave speeches at rallies.

*Freedom* covered not only the situation of African Americans but also the ongoing struggles of liberation against European colonialism in Africa itself. Hansberry's sophisticated awareness of African history and civilization was brought to bear in stories she wrote about the democratic African heroes Jomo Kenyatta of Kenya and Kwame Nkrumah of Ghana. During these activist days in New York, she took an advanced seminar in African history at the Jefferson School of Social Science under W.E.B. Du Bois, then in his eighties and just ten years before his ultimate expatriation to Ghana, where he would finally die in 1963.

This African emphasis in Hansberry's self-awareness was unusual in the 1950s and important because it would ultimately be expressed through the Nigerian character Joseph Asagai in *Raisin*. Back in Wisconsin she had started writing a college novel about a black undergraduate woman having a romance with an African exchange student and its impact on her identity and self-image, very much like Beneatha and Asagai. She had called it *All the Dark and Beautiful Warriors*. Africa would always remain an inspiration:

> *Beauty* . . . stark and full. . . .
>
> No *part* of something this—but rather, Africa, simply Africa. These thighs and arms and flying winged cheekbones, these hallowed eyes—without negation or apology. . . .
>
> *A classical people demand a classical art.*[15]

As with her interest in Africa, going back to her scholar uncle, there had been long and thoughtful preparation for this role of political activist in Hansberry's previous experience. She had been chairman of a radical student group in college, before which she had absorbed her father's activist legacy through his own example and from the articulate, socially committed guests such as Robeson and Du Bois, whose conversation she had heard at her family dinner table as a child. In fact, Robeson had just taken over *Freedom* as publisher, and Du Bois was a regular contributor and a guiding spirit.

## THE WORLD OF THE COLD WAR

But following World War II, the political landscape had shifted. The Soviet Union was no longer a U.S. ally but its cold war enemy. And fear of Communist treason created blacklists and persecution associated with the name of Senator Joseph McCarthy. Du Bois's increasing disaffection from American democracy was making it hard for him to secure teaching positions, and Robeson's open admiration for the Soviet Union was perceived as dangerous. Although Robeson denied being a Communist when questioned by the House Un-American Activities Committee (HUAC) in 1946, he refused to reaffirm the denial two years later, and he suggested that African Americans should not fight in a war against the Soviet Union. When the Korean War broke out in 1950 and Robeson publicly spoke against it, his passport was revoked by the government.

Thus, when Hansberry committed herself to Robeson's brand of radicalism, she knowingly embraced hardship and risk. Writing to a friend about "foul" fascism, she said, "Many . . . have already been lapped up by this new Reich terror. . . . Know the arrests in the early morning, the shifty-eyed ones who follow, follow, follow . . . and know the people who are the victims: the quiet and the courageous."[16] When Robeson was invited to address an international peace conference in Montevideo, Uruguay, in 1952, he wrote a speech denouncing the Korean War but was unable to give it because, lacking a passport, he could not travel internationally. Hansberry flew to Uruguay as his representative, gave the speech, and promptly had her own passport revoked. Despite this, her political commitment remained strong: "I would recall the horsemen I have seen riding down human beings in Times Square because they were protesting lynching. . . . I am sick of poverty, lynching, stupid wars and the universal maltreatment of my people and obsessed with a rather desperate desire for a new world for me and my brothers."[17]

## PARTNERS IN COMMITMENT

Hansberry's commitment was shared by Robert Nemiroff, whom she had met on a picket line demanding the integration of the New York University basketball team. A romance had blossomed between them, despite Nemiroff's being white, and in 1953 they were married at the Hansberry home in Chicago. Both families were fully represented and approving. The bride and groom had been up most of the night before their wedding at a demonstration protesting the execution of Soviet spies Julius and Ethel Rosenberg. The newlyweds agreed on their priorities. Nemiroff's political commitment became one with his personal commitment to his wife and her writing career.

The couple moved into an apartment in Greenwich Village, one of the more hospitable neighborhoods in New York for an interracial couple in the 1950s. With this shift began a period of transition between her activism and writing. The political commitment she felt did not diminish, but the form of it changed. She came to feel that she needed more time to write and that literary writing rather than journalism was the way she could best help bring about social change. On a long Christmas train trip back to Chicago by herself, she pondered her changing roles and came to the conclusion that, first and foremost, "I am a writer."[18]

While Hansberry continued to write articles for *Freedom*, including a glowing tribute to Robeson in 1954, she gave up the traveling and the grueling hours of full-time work at the magazine. Instead she took less demanding jobs—as a typist, an assembly-line worker in the fur district, a group leader in a home for the handicapped, and a theatrical assistant—that would allow her more time to work on the three plays she had started to write.

## A FULL-TIME WRITER

But the transition from activist to writer was not complete until three years later, in 1956, when Nemiroff and a friend wrote a popular song called "Cindy, Oh, Cindy," which provided a windfall of one hundred thousand dollars that allowed Hansberry to devote herself to writing full time. Energized by this good fortune, she embraced the role of writer as fully as she had that of activist and worked intensely on one of her three plays. Set in the South Side of Chicago where she had grown up, the play was about a family carrying on after the father's death and deciding how to honor his legacy, just as her family had. However, this was not an upper-middle-class family but rather a working-class one, the kind she had admired since grade school. After eight months of work, the first draft of *A Raisin in the Sun* was finished.

One evening Hansberry read the new play to a dinner guest, music publisher Philip Rose. Rose immediately and enthusiastically committed himself to producing the play with a live cast of actors onstage—and not in a church basement but on Broadway. Not only would that be an expensive undertaking, but it would also be unprecedented to have a serious drama by and about real African Americans in the American theater.

Rose, Hansberry, and Nemiroff worked for more than a year to find a partner and raise the money for the production. They hired Lloyd Richards to direct and Sidney Poitier and Claudia McNeil to star in the play, as well as a talented young cast. When the play opened on Broadway on March 11, 1959, it was an instant success—with the critics and with black and white audiences alike. The play ran for 530 performances, and Columbia Pictures bought the film rights for three hundred thousand dollars. It agreed to keep the original cast and have Hansberry herself adapt the play for the screen.

## CELEBRITY

When *A Raisin in the Sun* received the prestigious New York Drama Critics' Circle Award as best play that season, it was a major event: Hansberry was distinguished in being not only the youngest writer but also the first African American ever to be so honored. In addition, she was only the fifth woman to win the award. For the past six years, she had been unable to earn a living writing. Now she was more than a successful writer; she was famous, and she was a celebrity, a role she hadn't even really considered.

Suddenly she was getting up to thirty pieces of mail a day, and she was trying to answer each of them. Her telephone was alive with requests for interviews and offers of writing projects. Sometimes she found herself attending events for three or four different organizations in a single day. Young writers and artists asked her to consider their work and perhaps endorse it. Hansberry would turn on the television news and see herself being interviewed.

Even the fashion magazine *Vogue* was able to adapt the newly famous Hansberry to its use: "Her writing clothes are still rather campus—white, beat sneakers, thick white socks, chino pants. At the New York opening of her play, however, she wore beautiful black with a rope of pearls."[19]

Two years later, Hansberry and Nemiroff bought a house at Croton-on-Hudson, New York, an hour north of the city, where she could get away from her own fame and work on several writing projects she had begun beyond the *Raisin* screenplay.

## PIONEER AND PROPHET

Once the superficial whirlwind of celebrity died down, it became clear that the cultural impact of the play was extraordinary. African American experience had never been so truly

explored in the theater, and African Americans were profoundly validated by it. Thus, Hansberry opened up one of
the most venerated cultural forms to African American experience as a subject. The play also deeply affected black
artists, and Hansberry opened up theater to African American artistry as a means. A black theater movement began
based on *Raisin* that recognized Hansberry as a cultural pioneer, a fourth role beyond her first three roles as activist,
writer, and celebrity. Producer-director Woodie King Jr. has
paid tribute to Hansberry for showing others the way:

> *A Raisin in the Sun* opened doors within my consciousness
> that I never knew existed. There I was in Detroit's Cass The-
> atre, a young man who had never seen anywhere a black man
> (Walter Lee) express all the things I felt but never had the
> courage to express—and in a theater full of black and white
> people, no less! . . . The power of the play had made us all
> aware of our uniqueness as Blacks and had . . . confirmed that
> our dreams were possible. . . . The effect all this had on the
> current crop of black artists is tremendous. . . . To mention all
> of the artists whose careers were enhanced by their encoun-
> ters with Hansberry and *A Raisin in the Sun* would read like
> a *Who's Who* in the black theater.[20]

Once Hansberry opened the door with *Raisin* in 1959, a flood
of African American theatrical talent and accomplishment
poured through in the following decades. Two prominent ex-
amples are the 1964 plays *Blues for Mr. Charlie* by James
Baldwin and *Dutchman* by LeRoi Jones (now Amiri Baraka),
both of which present African American experience and
black-white relations in a much harsher way than Hansberry
had in *Raisin*. In the 1970s several black women playwrights
such as Ntozake Shange and Adrienne Kennedy, taking their
inspiration from Hansberry, gained important recognition
for their plays. And the Pulitzer Prize–winning playwright
August Wilson is a major figure who emerged in the black
theater movement in the 1980s.

But Hansberry's cultural pioneering goes beyond the black
theater movement to her prophetic vision of the civil rights,
women's, and ethnic pride movements that would soon
transform American life. Historian Lerone Bennett Jr. says,
"She was a kind of herald, a person announcing the coming
of something."[21] *Raisin*'s title is a warning meant to alert society to the danger of a "dream deferred," as Langston
Hughes put it in his poem—such as the American dream put
on hold for blacks because of racism. In Hughes's image, the
sun just might cause a raisin to explode, as indeed the

ghettoes of Los Angeles, Newark, and Detroit did in self-destructive rioting beginning the summer after Hansberry's death.

## THE TARGET OF CRITICISM

Despite the distractions of success and celebrity, Hansberry researched and wrote *The Drinking Gourd*, a made-for-television play about slavery commissioned by NBC, during 1960, the year following *Raisin*. In addition to her library research on slavery, she reached back to memories of her grandmother as inspiration. The title refers to the Big Dipper constellation, which always points north and was thus used by runaway slaves riding the Underground Railroad as a guide to freedom. "Follow the Drinking Gourd" is an African American spiritual in which heaven is glimpsed as a liberation from slavery.

But NBC deemed the play too controversial and never produced it. Also in 1960, the first and second drafts of Hansberry's screenplay for *Raisin* were rejected by Columbia Pictures for being too creative and not close enough to her own original play. Hansberry, despite her status as a celebrity and cultural pioneer, was coming to be seen as a potentially dangerous figure by mainstream media of her day. Determined not to abdicate her role as an activist, she began writing two ambitious new plays: *Les Blancs*, about European colonialism in black Africa, and *The Sign in Jenny Reed's Window*, about political and social commitment among mostly white bohemians in Greenwich Village.

Hansberry returned to political activity as well, raising money for the newly formed Student Nonviolent Coordinating Committee (SNCC). In 1963 she was involved in a meeting between Attorney General Robert F. Kennedy and a small group of prominent artists and intellectuals, most of whom were black. Expecting a round of congratulations for the administration's support of civil rights, Kennedy instead was confronted with dissatisfaction with what was perceived as the administration's statements in place of action. It was Hansberry who had the personal courage and moral authority to confront Kennedy in such a way that he reportedly was unable to return her penetrating gaze. She then shook his hand politely and walked out of the meeting in protest—followed by writer James Baldwin, entertainers Lena Horne and Harry Belafonte, and the rest of the inspired conferees.

Given the extent of Hansberry's sudden fame as a celebrity, negative criticism was perhaps inevitable—

whether from jealousy or misunderstanding, or from legitimately perceived shortcomings in her work. In any case, she became a target of critics who accused her of being a "slumlord" because of her family's real estate business and a hypocrite for writing a play about slum dwellers. She was also accused of writing liberal propaganda for white audiences in order to show that black people were just like whites. According to these critics, the Youngers were merely white middle-class characters disguised as African Americans. Judged by the standard of the more militant plays such as Baraka's *Dutchman, Raisin* was viewed as a sellout of the real black experience.

In the 1960s this criticism stemmed in part from a split within the radical community along generational lines—between the "new left," those who were coming of age in the 1960s, and the "old left," those who had come of age in the 1930s like Paul Robeson. The new left disdained the old as overly intellectual, Soviet-oriented, and conservative. And Hansberry, like Robeson, was considered old left. So she was cast in the new role of target of criticism, both from conservative producers in the entertainment industry and from militant radicals. Regardless, she was determined to maintain two of her earlier roles—those of political activist and writer.

## A Fatal Illness

But something happened to Lorraine Hansberry in 1963: She got sick. Tests revealed the possibility of cancer, and exploratory surgery confirmed it. After two operations in June and August, she seemed to be regaining strength and was determined to continue with her work. When SNCC honored her by asking her to write the text for their official photographic record, *The Movement,* she accepted the project without hesitation.

A scene from *Les Blancs,* her African play, was staged at the Actors' Studio Writers Workshop, and Hansberry continued revising the play. She also revised *What Use Are Flowers?,* a short play about the few survivors of a nuclear war, written as a commentary on Samuel Beckett's modernist absurdist drama *Waiting for Godot.* While she was moved by Beckett's play, she felt that it challenged her belief in direct political action. Her rejoinder was this short play, not produced until 1994 in Atlanta. But her main focus in 1964 was the other play she had started, now called *The Sign in Sidney Brustein's Window,* about the need for moral and political commitment.

She had writing plans beyond *Sidney Brustein*—on such diverse subjects as her childhood hero Toussaint-Louverture, the Haitian liberator; Mary Wollstonecraft, the eighteenth-century British feminist writer; Peter LaFarge's Native American novel *Laughing Boy;* and Akhenaton, the monotheistic Egyptian pharaoh of the New Kingdom. However, the cancer returned and Hansberry suspected she would not get to these projects.

The stress of the illness, in addition to her celebrity and the political controversies surrounding her, took their toll on the Hansberry-Nemiroff marriage. While they continued to work together effectively as partners on behalf of Hansberry's writing career, they quietly and amicably obtained a divorce in 1964. As working partners, they prepared to present *Sidney Brustein* on Broadway.

Hansberry and her private nurse moved into a hotel near the theater so she could attend rehearsals of the play that she knew would be her final work. When *The Sign in Sidney Brustein's Window* opened on October 15, 1964, it got mixed reviews and was threatened with closing. Many well-known artists and writers—among them Lillian Hellman, Richard Rodgers, Shelley Winters, Steve Allen, and Mel Brooks—took part in a public campaign to support the play and keep it running. They managed to do so for 101 performances, until January 11, 1965, the day before Lorraine Hansberry died of cancer at the age of thirty-four.

Martin Luther King Jr. sent a message of condolence to the funeral that made quite a claim for Lorraine Hansberry: "Her creative literary ability and her profound grasp of the deep social issues confronting the world today will remain an inspiration to generations yet unborn."[22]

## LITERARY LIFE AFTER DEATH

Having gone from obscurity to instant celebrity with *Raisin,* Hansberry had become controversial and the object of harsh criticism. Her second major play was successful with neither the critics nor the general public. Initially after her death, Hansberry seemed to be forgotten.

But she chose her former husband as her literary executor, and although Robert Nemiroff's support as a partner and promoter was highly effective while she was alive, it was even more remarkable, paradoxically, after her death. Unable at first to generate much interest, Nemiroff was asked in 1967 for help with a Hansberry tribute planned by an FM radio station in New York. Rising to the occasion, he created a seven-hour program called *Lorraine Hansberry in Her Own Words.* It consisted of recordings of Hansberry speaking and of scenes from her plays featuring sixty-one of America's most distinguished actors, including Anne Bancroft, Lauren Bacall, Lee J. Cobb, Bette Davis, Julie Harris, James Earl Jones, Angela Lansbury, Sidney Poitier, Paul Robeson, and Cicely Tyson. The radio broadcasts sparked new excitement in Hansberry and her tragically shortened career.

Nemiroff then assembled these scenes and voice recordings along with selections from her unpublished autobiographical writings. The result was a kind of portrait of Hansberry in her own words, which Nemiroff coproduced off-Broadway as a play and later published as a book entitled *To Be Young, Gifted, and Black.* Both were extraordinarily successful, and Hansberry's earlier role as a cultural pioneer was thus revived.

Nemiroff was sufficiently energized on Hansberry's behalf to create a series of seven more projects over the remaining twenty-two years of his life. He finished writing *Les Blancs* and assisted in its production on Broadway, starring James Earl Jones (1970); he adapted and produced a new version of *The Sign in Sidney Brustein's Window* with music, as originally conceived by Hansberry (1972); and he edited *The Drinking Gourd* and *What Use Are Flowers?* and published them along with *Les Blancs* in the single-volume *Les Blancs: The Collected Last Plays of Lorraine Hansberry* (1972). Nemiroff also adapted and produced *Raisin* as a highly successful Broadway musical (1973); he created with Ernest Kaiser a complete bibliography of more than 250 published items by and about Hansberry and her works (1979); and he coproduced the "Twenty-Fifth Anniversary Revival" of *Raisin* (1986) and the television production starring Danny Glover (1989) based on it. As a final tribute, Nemiroff edited and published Hansberry's original screenplay for *Raisin* shortly before his own death in 1991.

The last two projects were received by critics and the public alike with enthusiasm and reverence. On February 1, 1989, the original PBS broadcast with Danny Glover received the highest Nielsen ratings among black viewers of any program ever shown on PBS, demonstrating that critics who claimed the play was for a white audience were on shaky ground. Most telling perhaps was the *Washington Post* review by Amiri Baraka, whose *Dutchman* had often been compared to *Raisin* as more black, more radical. Baraka wrote that neither his play nor Baldwin's *Blues for Mr. Charlie* "is as much a statement from the African-American majority as is *Raisin*." He admitted that he and other sixties radicals "missed the essence of the work. . . . There is no such thing as a 'white folks' neighborhood' except to racists and *to those submitting to racism.*"[23]

## TIMELESS AND PERMANENT

After twenty-five years, with the integrity of *Raisin* as a black play thus affirmed, critics turned their attention to it as a woman's play as well, and finally, as a classic American family drama dealing with such universal themes as the individual versus the family and the relationship between adult children and their parents. Hansberry was posthumously cast in her ultimate role—as a classic American playwright of the timeless stature of white male playwrights like Eugene O'Neill, Tennessee Williams, and Arthur Miller. And classic American playwright is appropriate as Lorraine Hansberry's final role because it incorporates and transcends all of her other roles.

## NOTES

1. Lorraine Hansberry, *To Be Young, Gifted and Black*, ed. Robert Nemiroff. New York: Random House, 1969, p. 66.
2. James Baldwin, "Sweet Lorraine," introduction to *To Be Young, Gifted and Black*, pp. xi–xii.
3. Hansberry, *To Be Young, Gifted and Black*, p. 53.
4. Hansberry, *To Be Young, Gifted and Black*, p. 50.
5. Jean Carey Bond, "Lorraine Hansberry: To Reclaim Her Legacy," *Freedomways*, 1979, p. 184.
6. Hansberry, *To Be Young, Gifted and Black*, p. 64.
7. Hansberry, *To Be Young, Gifted and Black*, p. 51.
8. Steven R. Carter, *Hansberry's Drama: Commitment amid Complexity*. Urbana: University of Illinois Press, 1991, p. 8.
9. Quoted in *New Yorker*, "The Talk of the Town," May 9, 1959, p. 34.
10. Quoted in "The Talk of the Town," p. 34.
11. Hansberry, *To Be Young, Gifted and Black*, p. 87.
12. Quoted in "The Talk of the Town," p. 34.
13. Hansberry, *To Be Young, Gifted and Black*, p. 93.
14. Hansberry, *To Be Young, Gifted and Black*, p. 97.
15. Hansberry, *To Be Young, Gifted and Black*, p. 106.
16. Hansberry, *To Be Young, Gifted and Black*, pp. 102–103.

17. Hansberry, *To Be Young, Gifted and Black*, p. 102.
18. Hansberry, *To Be Young, Gifted and Black*, p. 105.
19. Quoted in Hansberry, *To Be Young, Gifted and Black*, p. 125.
20. Woodie King Jr., "Lorraine Hansberry's Children: Black Artists and *A Raisin in the Sun*," *Freedomways*, 1979, pp. 219–22.
21. Lerone Bennett Jr. and Margaret C. Burroughs, "A Lorraine Hansberry Rap," *Freedomways*, 1979, p. 229.
22. Quoted in Hansberry, *To Be Young, Gifted and Black*, p. i.
23. Quoted in Lorraine Hansberry, *A Raisin in the Sun (Expanded Twenty-Fifth Anniversary Edition) and The Sign in Sidney Brustein's Window*, ed. Robert Nemiroff. New York: Plume, 1987, p. 20.

# CHARACTERS AND PLOT

The main characters in *A Raisin in the Sun* belong to the African American Younger household, an extended family of five members covering three generations. The Youngers are two separate branches of a family sharing one cramped tenement apartment in the ghetto on the South Side of Chicago in the 1950s. Walter Lee is the head of one branch of the family. He is a chauffeur in his midthirties who dreams of being a better provider for his hardworking and devoted wife, Ruth, and their ten-year-old son, Travis. Another branch within the household, however, is Walter's original family—headed by his mother, the recently widowed matriarch Lena (Mama). It includes his sister, the ambitious twenty-year-old college student Beneatha (Bennie), as well as Walter himself.

Walter's subordinate role as son/brother in his mother's family branch complicates his dominant role as father/husband in his own. At the same time, the limited economic opportunities for African Americans in the segregated United States of the 1950s further compromise his prospects as a provider. Both Ruth and Lena must work outside the home as domestics to pay the bills.

But as the play begins, the family is focused on an economic opportunity as they anticipate the imminent arrival of a ten-thousand-dollar life insurance payment for the death of Walter's father. They are considering a series of variations on the American dream: Lena wants to make a down payment on a house, Walter wants to open a retail business, and Bennie wants to go to medical school.

## THE PLAY'S TWO HEROES

As the one character who belongs to both branches of the family, and as the one who is transformed by the play's events and who leads the others in its finale, Walter is the central figure, the protagonist, of *Raisin*. "He finally come into his manhood today, didn't he? Kind of like a rainbow after the rain," says Mama in one of the play's closing lines, emphasizing Walter's heroism.

Yet Lena herself is such a strong character that Walter does not dominate the play, as a traditional dramatic hero would. "She is one of those women of a certain grace and beauty," Hansberry writes of Lena in the stage directions. "Her face is full of strength. . . . Her bearing is perhaps most like the noble bearing of the women of the Hereros of Southwest Africa." Any heroism of Walter's is a function of his empowerment by his mother, and indeed *Raisin* is dedicated "to Mama."

The play thus has two heroes, just as it has two branches of the Younger family crowded into one apartment. Hansberry herself considered it a flaw in *Raisin* that, as characters in the same play, Walter and Lena prevent each other from being its single larger-than-life focus.

## MINOR ROLES

Characters other than the Youngers include Beneatha's two suitors: the wealthy, assimilated African American snob George Murchison and the politically committed Nigerian exchange student Joseph Asagai. Clearly they represent extreme identity choices for Beneatha, especially in view of her rejection of Murchison, on the one hand, and Asagai's marriage proposal and offer to live and work in Nigeria, on the other.

Two more characters who are not significant in themselves deliver important messages: bad news that the Youngers' American dreams have become nightmares. Walter's friend Bobo brings the news that Walter has been swindled out of not only his own part of the insurance money but also Bennie's. Karl Lindner, a white man, comes to tell them that their new white neighbors want to keep the Youngers out of their community because they are black.

Mrs. Johnson is a nosy neighbor who makes one comic appearance, which was cut from the original production because of running time and the cost of an additional actor.

## TITLE AND EPIGRAPH

The phrase *a raisin in the sun* comes from the poem "Montage of a Dream Deferred" by the celebrated African American poet Langston Hughes (1902–1967). Hughes was a guest in the Hansberry home when Lorraine was a child, and later he was both a literary influence and a cultural hero for her as well. In a quotation from the Hughes poem that appears before the text of the play as an epigraph, and as part of the printed program at performances of *Raisin*, Hansberry offers a context for her title:

What happens to a dream deferred?
Does it dry up
Like a raisin in the sun?
Or fester like a sore—
And then run?
Does it stink like rotten meat?
Or crust and sugar over—
Like a syrupy sweet?

Maybe it just sags
Like a heavy load.

*Or does it explode?*

This vivid imagery suggests the persistence, power, and unpredictability of dreams, and it is a warning of the danger of deferring them—as the American dream has been deferred for African Americans by racism.

Walter speaks of his dreams in the play's very first scene, and later in the same scene we learn that his father was also a dreamer. Their dreams are about family and children: "Seem like God didn't see fit to give the black man nothing but dreams—but he did give us children to make them seem worth while," Lena quotes her late husband.

From Lena's point of view, the question of her son's behavior as a fulfillment or as a desecration of her dream is dramatically addressed as the play unfolds. Owning a family home was a dream of Big Walter's and Lena's that was deferred, ironically until his death. And home ownership was a deferred dream of Walter Lee and Ruth as well.

Bennie's dream of becoming a doctor despite both racial and gender barriers may be the most extreme dream of all. When this family of American dreamers submits to despair, it is the Nigerian Asagai who speaks for idealism in the face of suffering and death. Finally, the dedication of the play includes the phrase "*in gratitude for the dream.*" It is clear that Hansberry's purpose in *Raisin* is to affirm dreaming and idealism in the context of the most clear-eyed realism about failures and setbacks in the struggle.

## STRUCTURE AND THE THREE UNITIES

The first half of the play is focused on the arrival of the insurance money and the question of how to spend it. This gives the first half "unity of action." Along with this is "unity of time" in that these first three scenes take place within one twenty-four-hour period surrounding the money's arrival. The second half of the play begins with a transitional scene that finally resolves the first half of the play and the spending of the ten thousand dollars, while introducing the unified action of the second half: the Youngers' move to a white neighborhood, which takes place a few weeks later in its own unified time. Thus, *Raisin* divides itself into two halves, each unified by its own time and action. The whole play is unified by the dovetailing of the two actions, when Walter's management of the insurance money (first half action) threatens the move (second half action).

*Raisin* also observes the "unity of place," which helps focus and compress many traditional plays, since all six of the play's scenes take place in the central living space of the Youngers' apartment. This space is essential to the play's meaning in that it is overcrowded, run-down, and inadequate for the growing family. When the play begins, Ruth is pregnant again, but uneasily and secretly so because of the inadequacy of these living quarters, and she is considering an illegal abortion. The living/dining room where the play takes place is also where Travis sleeps at night; his grandmother and his aunt share the apartment's one bedroom (offstage), and his parents sleep in "a second room" (which in the beginning of the life of this apartment was probably a breakfast room). And all five family members have the inconvenience and indignity of a bathroom down the hall that they must share with neighbors. All of these qualities of the apartment are emphasized in the play's very first scene, almost as if the space is another character in the play.

### ACT 1, SCENE 1

The play begins at 7:30 on a Friday morning with a ringing alarm clock. Ruth wakes Travis from his bed on the couch and sends him out to the hall bathroom to start his day. Then Walter appears, his mind already fixed on the life insurance check he expects in the mail. After Travis leaves for school, Walter asks Ruth to help him persuade his mother to invest the insurance money in a liquor store. She is unenthusiastic, and he is frustrated.

Beneatha appears next, waiting for her turn in the bathroom. Sister and brother bicker about her ambition to be a doctor, which he resents because he knows his mother would rather spend money on medical school than on a liquor store. He tells her to become a nurse or get married. Walter leaves for work and finally Lena enters.

Out of loyalty to her husband and despite her own lack of enthusiasm for the idea, Ruth makes her plea to Lena for Walter's liquor store. Lena is not receptive. She is determined to put some money aside for Beneatha's schooling and is considering making a down payment on a house for the family. Lena reminisces about Big Walter, his dreams, his love for his children, and his despair at the death of their child Claude. She also remembers how he finally worked himself to death for his dreams and his children.

When Beneatha returns from the bathroom, the three women jokingly discuss her attempts to find herself through guitar lessons, horseback riding, and photography. They note her coolness toward her wealthy fellow student George Murchison and toward marriage itself. But when Bennie makes a disrespectful remark about God, Lena asserts her authority by slapping her daughter's face. Bennie submits resentfully, accusing her mother of tyranny as she leaves the room.

Lena laments the feeling of losing touch with her children while she tends her plant, which reminds her of them: "They spirited all right, my children. Got to admit they got spirit— Bennie and Walter. Like this little old plant that ain't never had enough sunshine or nothing—look at it." While Lena daydreams and looks out the window, Ruth faints because of her pregnancy.

## Act 1, Scene 2

The following morning, after Travis reports on the killing of a rat in the street, Ruth acknowledges to Lena and Beneatha that she is two months pregnant. Bennie confronts Ruth about the lack of space for a new family member, but she then apologizes. Ruth inadvertently reveals that she has gone to see an abortionist rather than an obstetrician, much to religious Lena's dismay.

Beneatha receives a visit from Joseph Asagai, the foreign exchange student, who brings her authentic Nigerian robes and records of Nigerian music. He also gives her the Yoruba name, Alaiyo, which he defines as "One for Whom Bread— Food—Is Not Enough." She is gratified by his recognition of her idealism.

When the ten-thousand-dollar check arrives in the mail,

Lena tells Walter, without any discussion, that she will not invest in any liquor store. She again asserts her authority and slaps him down with her refusal to consider his business proposal—as clearly as she had literally slapped Bennie's face in the first scene. He angrily accuses his mother of depriving his family by refusing him the chance to provide for them properly. Lena in turn challenges Walter to be a man worthy of his father, Big Walter, by saving his unborn child from Ruth's intended abortion.

When Walter is unable to speak and flees the apartment, Lena declares him "a disgrace to [his] father's memory."

## ACT 2, SCENE 1

Later the same day, Beneatha appears in her African robes, dancing to the Nigerian folk records Asagai has given her, with great comic effect. Walter arrives drunk and joins in the fun, fantasizing that he is a powerful African chieftain.

Suitor George Murchison arrives for a date with Beneatha. She reveals a close-cropped, unstraightened hairdo, unusual for African American women at that time, and gets a stunned reaction from everyone. (This was dropped from the original production when the unfamiliar hairdo was not effectively created for the actress playing Bennie.) When George mocks Beneatha's interest in African culture and history, she reacts with righteous indignation.

While George is waiting for Beneatha to get ready, Walter tries to engage him in conversation about his father's business, but George acts bored. Walter expresses his resentment of privileged college students like George, who then accuses Walter of bitterness and compares him to the Greek hero Prometheus. Walter does not understand the reference.

Later that evening as Walter and Ruth share an intimate moment, Lena abruptly enters, to Walter's embarrassment, and announces that she has made a down payment on a house in Clybourne Park. She tells Travis that it will eventually be his and that his grandfather got it for him. The fact that Clybourne Park is a white neighborhood gives the family pause, but only briefly. Lena explains that it was simply a matter of getting the best house available for the money they had.

Ruth is ecstatic about the new house. But when Lena asks Walter to affirm her decision to buy it, he accuses her of having "butchered up a dream of mine" and walks out, leaving her alone and "thinking heavily."

## ACT 2, SCENE 2

A few weeks later, as Beneatha is returning from a date with George Murchison, he becomes impatient with her conversation and her thinking; when he tries to become physically intimate instead, she sends him away. She tells Lena that George is a fool, and her mother affirms her, saying, "Well—I guess you better not waste your time with no fools." This is a dramatic reversal of the slap in the face she gave Bennie in the first scene. Even though Lena likes George as a potential husband for Bennie, especially since he is so well-off, she suspends her own judgment and supports her daughter. Bennie recognizes her mother's support and thanks her, "For understanding me this time."

Walter is drunk again and his job is in jeopardy. He has been skipping work and escaping reality by taking drives in the country, getting drunk, and losing himself in the music at a local bar called the Green Hat.

Later, near the end of this scene, Lena does something for Walter similar to what she did for Bennie by supporting her. She does this by giving Walter thirty-five hundred dollars to spend as he sees fit and another three thousand dollars to put aside for Beneatha's medical school. She recognizes that her refusal to support Walter's dreams has broken his spirit, and she has the humility to say, "I been wrong, son." Walter expresses his gratification in a final moment with Travis at the very end of the scene, when he delineates a scenario of their future prosperity now that he has been given a chance to earn it.

During her heavy thinking, Lena apparently realized that her thirty-five-year-old son and twenty-year-old daughter were too old to be controlled by her. Her heroism as a loving parent is her ability to see the harmfulness of her authority as her children get older. She is heroic in her willingness to empower them even when she knows they may use the authority she gives them in ways she does not approve of. Thus, the first half of the play ends with Lena empowering her children after disempowering them in the first two scenes.

In between the affirmations of Bennie at the beginning of this scene and Walter at the end is the comic visit from the neighbor Mrs. Johnson. This pivotal scene resolves the first half of the play by determining the final disposition of the ten thousand dollars. It also initiates the second half of the play when Mrs. Johnson warns the Youngers, with barely dis-

guised glee, that in moving to a white neighborhood they are
going into a dangerous, possibly life-threatening, situation.

## ACT 2, SCENE 3

One week later it is moving day, and the mood is celebratory.
Walter, Ruth, and Bennie party while they pack. But their ju-
bilation is interrupted when Karl Lindner comes to the door,
representing the neighborhood organization where the
Youngers are moving. He politely offers on behalf of the organization to buy the Youngers' new house so that the neighborhood may remain all-white. Indignant, Walter asks him to
leave.

When Lena and Travis arrive immediately after, Bennie
and Walter joke about the buyout offer, and the upbeat mood
returns. Lena is given gifts of gardening tools from the adults
and a hat from Travis to celebrate the new house. They are
interrupted yet again, this time by Walter's friend Bobo. He
has come to tell Walter that Willy Harris, their partner in the
proposed liquor store, has stolen their money. In the humiliation of this disaster, Walter reveals that he has lost Beneatha's money as well as his own.

Crying, he crumples to the floor, with no shred of manhood or dignity left, and Lena loses control as she bemoans
the waste of all that Walter Sr. had worked for.

## ACT 3

An hour later, despair hangs over the apartment, and Asagai
arrives to help with the moving. His good cheer is jarringly
out of place, and Beneatha tells him about the loss of the
money. Agitated, she laments losing her dream to be a doctor
and recalls the incident from childhood that inspired her
professional ambition and the idealistic desire to help others.
Now nothing seems worth the effort. She mocks Asagai's
commitment to the liberation of his homeland and the establishment of a just society there: "You with all your talk and
dreams about Africa! You still think you can patch up the
world. Cure the Great Sore of Colonialism . . . with the Penicillin of Independence—!"

Asagai patiently explains how no setback can diminish his
activism. If he himself is seen to be a detriment to the better-
ment of his people, he will accept his own death as part of his
commitment. (This speech was drastically cut in the original
production because of concerns about pacing.) Asagai pro-
poses marriage to Beneatha and offers to take her back to

Nigeria to be a doctor. He asks her to take some time to think about it, and then he leaves.

Despite the offer, Bennie rages at Walter and his pretensions of being a businessman. Even strong Lena has fallen into despair and intends to cancel the move. Though Ruth still wants to move, she is near hysteria. Walter announces that he has invited Karl Lindner, the neighborhood association representative, to the apartment because he intends to accept the buyout offer as a way of recouping the stolen money.

When Lena objects that their family is too proud to take money for being told they are not fit to live among, Walter mocks the idea of their dignity, boasting recklessly of his willingness to disgrace himself and his people for money. And when he leaves and Bennie expresses her disgust with him, Lena reminds her that love is most crucial when a person "is at his lowest and can't believe in hisself 'cause the world done whipped him so!"

Lindner arrives, and Lena insists that Walter transact his business in front of his son so that Travis can understand what his family is about. So Walter begins by referring to their pride and, despite his announced intention to sell out the family, ends by dramatically telling Lindner that they have decided not to accept the buyout after all. They will move into their new house "because my father . . . earned it for us brick by brick."

The family is thrilled with Walter's spontaneous assertion of manhood that transcends money and worldly power. He provides his son with self-esteem and pride in his family and their dreams. Tough times are ahead for the Youngers as they move into a neighborhood that does not want them, but their commitment to working for dreams is intact. As the play ends and the Youngers vacate their old, shabby apartment, Lena makes sure to take along her plant, the symbol of her children and her nurturing of them.

# CHAPTER 1

# An African American Play

READINGS ON
A RAISIN IN THE SUN

# A Celebration of Black Life

Steven R. Carter

Steven R. Carter is the author of a major critical
work on Lorraine Hansberry, entitled Hansberry's
Drama: Commitment amid Complexity. He is a professor of African, African American, and Caribbean
literature at the University of Puerto Rico.

Carter's selection discusses the diversity of black
culture–through the generations and across conti-
nents–as portrayed in Raisin. In depicting West
African history and culture, A Raisin in the Sun
touches on the struggle for liberation from colonialism, authentic dress, and music. And in depicting
African American history and culture, it touches on
the migration from southern plantations to northern
cities, the evolution from segregation to integration,
and authentically American music forms such as
spirituals, blues, and jazz. Though distinct, both cultures share a strong bond in their histories and a
unity in their attempts to overcome oppression.
Raisin serves to bridge the gap between them as
Hansberry celebrates both cultures rather than one
at the expense of the other.

A Raisin in the Sun ringingly celebrates both black culture
and black resistance to white oppression through many generations. As Hansberry said, "The thing I tried to show was
the many gradations even in one Negro family, the clash of
the old and new, but most of all the unbelievable courage of
the Negro People." The three generations of the Younger
family depicted in the play differ in dreams, speech patterns,
and religious, musical, and stylistic preferences within the
African-American and African traditions, thus displaying the
richness and diversity in black culture. Yet they are unified

in their heroic defiance of white hostility and threats. Integration is not the issue. Rather, the test that the Youngers face is of their willingness to take potentially fatal risks to get out of an intolerable situation and to force change upon an oppressive system. . . .

Hansberry's craftsmanship in plotting thus served as a kind of rocket-launching base for her artistic explorations of the complexity of black culture, the strength of black resistance through many generations, and the extraordinariness of the most seemingly insignificant among them. She knew, of course, that her play had universal dimensions, but she also knew that they had to exist in a profound and fruitful tension with specific ones or her artistry would be unbalanced and all meaning skewed. In a 1959 interview with Studs Terkel in which she disputed the contention that her play was so universal that it could have been "about anyone" Hansberry observed "that one of the most sound ideas in dramatic writing is that, in order to create the universal, you must pay very great attention to the specific. In other words, I've told people that not only is [the Younger family] a Negro family, specifically and definitely and culturally, but it's not even a New York family, or a Southern Negro family. It is specifically about Southside Chicago.". . .

By juxtaposing Beneatha's desire to return to a purely African tradition with the wholehearted involvement of her mother and sister-in-law in African-American culture, Hansberry further delineated the diversity of black culture as well as made telling use of the opportunity to display the richness of both these major strands of it. . . .

### AN INTERCONTINENTAL BOND

Hansberry's dual aim of demonstrating that the African heritage of black Americans is a glorious one and "that the ultimate destiny and aspirations of the African people and twenty million American Negroes are inextricably and magnificently bound up together forever," is fulfilled in a variety of ways in *A Raisin in the Sun.* For example, she delightedly indicates the linkage in the stage direction, noting that Lena's "bearing is perhaps most like the noble bearing of the women of the Hereros of Southwest Africa." Beneatha's apparent willingness at the end of the play to entertain Asagai's proposal that she go to live with him in Africa suggests a symbolic as well as a personal link between blacks of America and those of Africa. In addition, Beneatha's intense reaction against anything smacking of white-washed American culture, prompted in part by Asagai's "teasing" remark that her straightened hair reflects the "assimilationism" of American blacks—a remark that she takes more seriously than he intends—leads her to change to an Afro hairstyle, wear the African dress that Asagai has given her, play African music on the record player, and attempt an African dance, thereby introducing audiences to the beauty of all these vital aspects of African tradition.

Walter's drunken decision to join his sister in fantasizing about being African provides a comic interlude that has serious overtones, especially in regard to his relation to Africa. His first words upon taking on the role of African are, significantly, "YEAH . . . AND ETHIOPIA STRETCH FORTH HER HANDS AGAIN! . . ." These words held a special meaning for Hansberry, as she explained to Harold Isaacs in an interview included in his book *The New World of Negro Americans:* "Why ever since I was three years old, . . . I knew that somebody somewhere was doing something to hurt black and brown peoples. Little as I was I remember the newsreels of the Ethiopian war and the feeling of outrage in our Negro community. Fighters with spears and our people in a passion over it; my mother attacking the Pope blessing the Italian troops going off to slay Ethiopians. . . . But we just expected that things would change. We had been saying for a long time: 'Ethiopia will stretch forth her hands!' This always meant that *they* were going to pay for all this one day."

In his imagination, Walter then becomes one of those "fighters with spears" and starts "actively spearing enemies all over the room." Moreover, he confirms his support for anti-colonialist struggle, like the one with which Asagai is involved in Nigeria, by saying, "Me and Jomo. . . . That's my man, Kenyatta," a pointed reference because Kenyatta had recently been imprisoned by the Kenyan colonial government for agitating for independence. Stage directions inform us that Walter *"sees what we cannot, that he is a leader of his people, a great chief, a descendent of Chaka."* In this context, it is important to note that the Zulu leader Chaka (also spelled Shaka), according to Mazisi Kunene in his introduction to *Emperor Shaka the Great,* initiated the "military machinery" that "brought about, fifty years later, one of the most dramatic defeats the British army suffered in all its colonial history." All of this is a reminder, as is Walter's subsequent speech calling his tribe to prepare for war, that African tribal culture was built around hunters and warriors whose spirits live on in Walter despite the shackling of his ambition and aggressiveness by American society. The poetic language Walter utters in his imaginary speech, differing widely from his everyday speech, is the kind he would have used as a leader in Africa, its eloquence highlighting that of the oral traditions of Africans. Hansberry again places the potential alongside the existing, thereby consciously expanding our conception of the "real."

The arrival of George Murchison for his date with Beneatha, and his distaste for what he regards as her reversion to the primitive, afford Hansberry another chance to comment on African culture. George's speech derogating Beneatha's views on the African heritage actually provides much positive information about Africa that Hansberry wished to place before audiences: "In one second we will hear all about the great Ashanti empires; the great Songhay civilizations; and the great sculpture of Bénin—and then some poetry in the Bantu—and the whole monologue will end with the word *heritage! (Nastily)* Let's face it, baby, your heritage is nothing but a bunch of raggedy-assed spirituals and some grass huts."

Moreover, Beneatha, while being comically pushed out of the room by her sister-in-law, manages to get in the last word: "GRASS HUTS! . . . See there . . . you are standing there in your splendid ignorance talking about people who were the first to smelt iron on the face of the earth! . . . The Ashanti were performing surgical operations when the English . . . were still tatooing themselves with blue dragons!"

Finally, as Hansberry remarked in her interview with Terkel, she viewed Asagai as representative of "the emergence of an articulate and deeply conscious colonial intelligentsia in the world." Hansberry further observed that "he also signifies a hangover of something that began in the '30s, when Negro intellectuals first discovered the African past and became very aware of it." She emphasized that she was referring not to Garveyism,[1] but to the intense interest and pride in the African past shown by the Harlem Renaissance

1. Black activist Marcus Garvey believed that African Americans could regain their self-respect by taking pride in black history. But he also advocated that social change for blacks was only going to come from self-help and separation from white society.

writers. As she stated, "I mean particularly in poetry and the creative arts. I want to reclaim it. Not physically—I don't mean I want to move there—but this great culture that has been lost may very well make decisive contributions to the development of the world in the next few years."

## EDUCATING HER READERS

Like Langston Hughes, Countee Cullen, and other Harlem Renaissance writers, Hansberry attempted to overcome the stereotyped image of Africans as perhaps one small step above apes and to present them as they really were. As shown by her portrayals of the ignorance of both Lena and George Murchison, she knew that probably as many American blacks as whites needed to be educated about the achievements and values of Africans. In fact, American blacks needed such information even more than did whites because their self-images and self-understanding depended in part upon it. Even so, she sought to avoid the romanticization and exoticism of the Harlem Renaissance because a self-image built on a base of falsity easily crumbles. Her figure of Asagai was probably a composite of many Africans whom she met at the university, the *Freedom* offices, and the Jefferson School for Social Science, where she had studied African history and culture under [scholar and activist] W.E.B. DuBois. She had also acquired an appreciation of Africa at an early age from her uncle William Leo Hansberry, the highly respected Africanist who had taught such future leaders of emerging African nations as Nnamdi Azikewe of Nigeria and Kwame Nkrumah of Ghana. No matter what sources she drew upon for the creation of Asagai, however, it was accurate enough to prompt Ezekiel Mphahlele, a self-exiled South African writer living in Nigeria, to remark in his study *The African Image* that "the Nigerian character and the image he represents of his people are so beautifully drawn without a condescending or patronizing tone."

Despite all her respect for the African past, Hansberry was even more concerned about the potential African contribution to the future. In response to a question from radio interviewer Patricia Marks concerning Beneatha's looking to Africa for a sense of identity, Hansberry commented:

> I think that Negro intellectuals and Negro artists are profoundly attracted once again. But this rebirth of that feeling has to do with the reassertion of the possibility that what we

currently call the western world is not necessarily the universe and perhaps we must take a more respectfull view of
the fact that African leaders today say that with regard to Europe and European traditions in the world that we will take
the best of what Europe has produced and the best of what
we have produced and try to create a superior civilization out
of the synthesis. I agree with them and I think that it commands respect for what will be inherently African in the contribution.

Asagai, with his Western education and his strong and loving sense of the traditions of his people, is clearly the kind of
African leader Hansberry described. He intends to bring
many changes to his village, seeking to eliminate the "illiteracy and disease and ignorance," but he feels that the ultimate judges of his actions must be his "black countrymen"
and that if he does something profoundly detrimental to
their way of life they would be justified in slitting his "then
useless throat."

## AFRICAN-AMERICAN MUSICAL EXPRESSION

Even though she praised the African past through Beneatha's
comments and Walter's drunken speech and the African present and future through the idealistic stance of Asagai, Hansberry never intended to glorify African culture at the expense of
African-American culture. By taking this position, she set herself apart from her character Beneatha, who is largely but not
entirely modeled on her creator. Like Ruth, Hansberry greatly
enjoyed the blues, which Beneatha, wholly immersed in her
newfound passion for all things African, dismisses "with an ar-
rogant flourish" as "assimilationist junk," and she also deeply
appreciated spirituals and jazz. For example, comparing the
contributions to posterity of Southern plantation-owners and
their slaves before the Civil War in an unpublished section of
her essay on "The New Paternalists," Hansberry contended that
"It is true . . . that all the wistful wishfulness of a nation notwith-
standing, the old slavocracy produced absolutely nothing worth
retaining in human culture, neither in science, art nor music,
in any measure comparable to what its slaves created—those
glorious subtleties of movement and imagery, harmony and
rhythm, of such portent that they not only survived but continue to nourish and re-vitalize the only native music our nation has brought forth.". . .

Hansberry . . . recognized that the Africans brought to
America as slaves and their variously oppressed descen-

## ASAGAI: AFRICAN SPOKESMAN FOR DIGNITY, SANITY, AND PROGRESS

*Alex Haley is the author of* The Autobiography of Malcolm X *and* Roots, *two landmark works of black literature. Here he comments on Hansberry's influence on American awareness of African reality, and how the character Asagai represented a new and positive image of black Africans.*

The list of Hansberry's contributions is lengthy, but one thing in particular has always struck me as unique, perhaps due to my own special interest in this subject. She wasn't the *first* black writer to illuminate the relationship between the American Black and Africa (that credit belongs to the Harlem Renaissance writers), but she was the first to *popularize* the notion. Merely by the force of *A Raisin in the Sun*'s success, she helped to dispel the myth of the "cannibal" African with a bone in his hair. Her educated African character, Asagai, was certainly the first time a large audience had seen and heard an African portrayed as carrying himself with dignity and as being, moreover, a primary spokesman for sanity and progress. It must also have been the first time a mass audience had ever seen a black woman gracefully don African robes or wear an "afro" hairstyle.

Alex Haley, "The Once and Future Vision of Lorraine Hansberry," *Freedomways*, (1979), pp. 278–79.

dents were forced to respond to the unique conditions they lived under here, conditions that necessarily led to the development of a culture along different lines from those in Africa. In fact, she gloried in the bruising and bravery that went into the creation of this culture. However . . . she also affirmed that the African component remains vitally important to African-American culture. . . .

Hansberry considered African-American music a central part of African-American culture. In her 1959 speech on "The Negro Writer and His Roots," made shortly before *A Raisin in the Sun* was produced on Broadway, she inveighed against those who sought to belittle both African-American music and its creators:

It was true thirty years ago and it is still true today that the soaring greatest of the spirituals begin and end in some minds as the product of religious childishness; they do not hear, even yet, in the "black and unknown bards" of whom James Weldon Johnson sang, the enormous soul of a great and incredibly courageous people who have known how to acknowledge pain and despair as one hope. In jazz rhythms, alien minds find only symbols for their own confused and mistaken yearnings for a return to primitive abandon; Norman Mailer writes, "For jazz is orgasm; it is the music of orgasm, good orgasm and bad. . . ." They do not hear as yet the tempo of an impatient and questioning people. Above all, in the murmur of the blues, they believe they know communion with naked sexual impulses peculiar to imperfect apes or noble savages; they miss the sweet and sad indictment of misery that forms that music. They "done taken our blues and gone."

This viewpoint underlies Hansberry's treatment of spirituals, jazz, blues, and other aspects of African-American culture throughout *A Raisin in the Sun*. In every mood, the musical part of their heritage speaks to the Youngers and reminds them what other blacks have felt, endured, and triumphed over.

As the embodiments of courage and strength, spirituals play a prominent role in the lives of the Youngers. When Lena feels depressed, she asks Ruth to "sing that 'No Ways Tired'" because "that song always lifts me up so—." Ruth herself turns to this song on the morning her family is about to leave the apartment she loathes for the white-encircled house she desires (with just a touch of dread):

> *Ruth's voice, a strident, dramatic church alto, cuts through the silence.*
> *It is, in the darkness, a triumphant surge, a penetrating statement of expectation:*
> "Oh, Lord, I don't feel no ways tired! Children, oh, glory hallelujah!"

Even Walter, in a moment when everything seems to be going his way, finds a spiritual the most appropriate means of expressing his sense of freedom and exuberance: "I got wings . . . you got wings . . . All God's children got wings . . ."

Jazz, as Hansberry indicated in her speech, is keyed to impatience and questioning. When Walter seeks release from the torment of his mother's refusal to give him money for a partial down payment on a liquor store and his wife's undesired pregnancy, he finds it in the music of a "little cat . . . who blows a sax" with a combo at the Green Hat bar. What Beneatha turns her back on when she seeks a purely African form of expression is, ironically, the blues. "A rather exotic saxophone blues" also serves as an ironic commentary on the scene in which the family sprays their apartment for cockroaches.

Hansberry also touches on another part of the African-American musical heritage by having Walter and Ruth, in a relaxed moment together, dance "a classic, body-melding 'slow drag.'" In the first published version of the play, the stage directions indicate that they "deliberately burlesque an old social dance of their youth." However, this scene, as originally conceived, involved a far more elaborate display of the diverse strands of African-American culture than either set of directions suggest. In the earlier, unproduced, and unpublished version, Walter enters the room singing an "old blues" in a "lusty manner" that is "a composite imitation of all the great old blues singers who occur to him": "Pretty Mama!/ . . . Throw me in your big—brass bed./ . . . Make love to me, mama, 'til my face turns che-ery red!" He then convinces Ruth to join him in burlesquing "the old 'Warwick' style social dance of their youth—cheek to cheek; torsos poked out behind." When Beneatha teases them about being "old-fashioned Negroes," Walter responds: "She don't think we dignified . . . That's right, this is the age of the *New Negro!* Today you got to croon in such a way as can't nobody tell you from the white boys!" Afterward, he does a string of imitations, beginning with Billy Eckstine (for which he twists "his head on his neck in the manner of the pretty-boy crooners") and moves on to Johnny Mathis, Nat "King" Cole, and Sammy Davis. Ruth is prompted to mimic "the Divine Sarah" Vaughn, Lena Horne, and Pearl Bailey, and even Beneatha, "finally overcome with the spirit of the nonsense," joins in, "turning and assuming the catcrouch, squinted eyes and guitar-voiced tones of Miss Kitt." Thus, by the time Lena and Travis return and bring them back to earth, all three have amply demonstrated their sophisticated appreciation of the rich variety of African-American cultural styles. Although the scene was much too lengthy and was rightly condensed in the final script, it shows Hansberry's meticulousness toward the cultural background of her characters—and her not always reverent delight in the variety of accomplishments by other blacks.

### AFRICAN-AMERICAN STEREOTYPES

In contrast, when Walter thinks about accepting Lindner's offer and thereby betrays his racial pride, he expresses the decision through the inauthentic, white-created form of the minstrel show and the stereotyped movie images of blacks derived from it. In response to his mother's question about how he will feel if he accepts the insulting offer of money,

Walter insists that he will feel fine and tells her further that he will get down on his "black knees" and say "Captain, Mistuh, Bossman. . . . A-hee-hee-hee! . . . Yasssssuh! Great white . . . Father, just gi' ussen de money, fo' God's sake, and we's—we's ain't gwine come out deh and dirty up yo' white folks neighborhood . . ."

The stage directions indicate that while he makes this speech he is "grovelling and grinning and wringing his hands in profoundly anguished imitation of the slow-witted movie stereotype." As Daniel J. Leab observes in *From Sambo to Superspade: The Black Experience in Motion Pictures,* the depiction of blacks

> in early American movies . . . was probably influenced most profoundly by the treatment of the black on stage and in the minstrel shows and vaudeville. The minstrel shows—whose performers appeared with faces darkened by sooty burnt-cork makeup—followed an elaborate ritual in their burlesque of Negro life in the Old South. Already well-established before the Civil War, they succeeded in fixing the black man in the American consciousness as a ludicrous figure supposedly born, as one show business history puts it, "hoofing on the levee to the strumming of banjos." He was prone to frenzied dancing, shiftlessness, garish dress, gin tippling, dice shooting, torturing the language, and, inevitably, was addicted to watermelon and chicken, usually stolen.

In performing his imitation of the stereotype, Walter uses the language of the burnt-cork "blacks" as described by Gerald Bradley: "In the beginning was the darkie, chirping 'Yassuh' and 'Nosuh' and 'Ahse gwine down to the sprink house 'n' ead me some waddemelon.'" By outwardly accepting the debasing stereotype, even though he inwardly disavows it, Walter implicitly supports Lindner's and his fellow whites' chief justification for their treatment of blacks. Moreover, his support extends to the full three centuries of lying and the oppression of his people. As Hansberry argued in her article "Me Tink Me Hear Sounds in de Night," the basic reason why "buffoonery or villainy was [the black's] only permissible role in the halls of entertainment or drama" for all that time was "a modern concept of racism" created by European slave-traders seeking "to render the African a 'commodity' in the minds of white men."

In contrast, when Walter turns his back on this false white-created tradition and stands up to Lindner, he brings along with him the true, life-sustaining traditions of his people embodied in his religious, spiritual-loving mother, his wife who turns to the blues for sustenance, and his sister who finds strength in African history and culture, including African music. Moreover, as Hansberry's great artistry has made abundantly clear, he himself, in speaking his own African-American idiom instead of a comic or exotic travesty of it, and in previously demonstrating a command of authentic African oratory, is a living embodiment of the multifaceted culture of his people. . . .

### CULTURAL DIVERSITY

*A Raisin in the Sun* is first and foremost a celebration of black life, with all its diversity and creativity in speech, music, and other cultural forms, and of black strength through generations in survival and struggle. Like Alex Haley's *Roots*, published seventeen years later, the play depicts black values being passed on from generation to generation, with each generation adding its own contribution but retaining the wisdom and will-to-freedom of its predecessors. In addition, it offers a vision of young and old, men and women, religious people and atheists, coming together on the basis of familial and community concern, recognition of common problems and the need for common action.

# Hansberry's Strategy
# for Racial Integration

Helene Keyssar

Helene Keyssar is the author of *The Curtain and the Veil*, a major work on black drama from which this selection comes. She discusses Hansberry's attempts to change white audiences' minds about blacks, whose daily lives were previously not visible to them. Hansberry believed that whites would fear blacks less upon seeing that the Younger family was similar to their own in many ways. Hence *Raisin* makes use of theatrical devices that are familiar to white American audiences: an easy-to-understand predicament and tension until the predicament is resolved late in the play. Since the predicament is also familiar to white Americans, there would be little resistance to *Raisin*'s characters, who are generally likable, funny, and clever. The play's humor is, in part, intended to relieve anxiety in white audiences about the black family onstage.

The success of *A Raisin in the Sun* is important to the history of black drama; it is also notable in a larger historical context. *A Raisin in the Sun* is the best known of the black dramas that transform into theatrical terms the political strategy of integration. The play includes only one white person in its cast, and this person, Mr. Lindner, appears in only two brief scenes; yet *A Raisin in the Sun* is vividly a drama of "contact of black and white." Hansberry's strategy is an attempt to reveal to the white audience how much black and white people really are alike; she wants the audience to desire the fulfillment of the personal dreams of the characters of the play. If white spectators can acknowledge both this likeness and the aspirations of the characters, they can abolish their fears; black and white people might then live to-

Excerpted from Helene Keyssar, *The Curtain and the Veil: Strategies in Black Drama* (New York: Burt Franklin, 1981). Reprinted by permission of the author.

gether harmoniously. Because white people are not ordinarily in situations through which they can see the daily lives of black people, the play will provide this experience. Black spectators will find nothing seductive in the presentation of black characters living out their lives, but the play can provide the pleasure and the terror of a rare instance of public acknowledgment that this place and these people are important. . . .

## FADED DREAMS

There can be little dispute concerning what *A Raisin in the Sun* is about: The play dramatizes the efforts and frustrations of a family in pursuit of the American dream. The title of the play is itself an allusion to this theme. "A raisin in the sun" is an image drawn from a Langston Hughes poem that presents the basic rhetorical questions apparent in Hansberry's play. Hughes's poem, taken from the volume *Montage of a Dream Deferred*, is almost an outline of the events enacted in *A Raisin in the Sun:*

> What happens to a dream deferred?
> Does it dry up
> Like a raisin in the sun?
> And fester like a sore—
> And then run?
> Does it stink like rotten meat?
> Or crust and sugar over—
> Like a syrupy sweet?
>
> Maybe it just sags
> Like a heavy load.
> *Or does it explode?*

Perceived as a poem about black people, Hughes's verse takes on particular concrete meanings, just as the black characters of Hansberry's play specify the elements of the plot because of their racial identities. There is little question, however, that the substantive center of both works is simply a description of what happens to a dream deferred.

In *A Raisin in the Sun* what happens to the deferred dream is just as Hughes imagines it. The Younger family of Hansberry's play are industrious, working-class Chicago black people. The sixty-year-old matriarch of the family, Mrs. Younger (Mama), came north with her husband years before the play begins in order to fulfill the American dream for her children. Although the family has survived except for Mr. Younger, who died of overwork, dreams of leisure and prosperity have almost dried up when the play begins. Walter Lee Younger, Mrs. Younger's thirty-five-year-old son, has been working for years as a chauffeur and is disgusted with his demeaning labor and his inability to go into business for himself; his wife, Ruth, is weary of her work as a domestic but is most deeply troubled by her sagging marriage, which she bears "like a heavy load." (Hansberry exploits Hughes's line: Early in the play we discover that Ruth is pregnant.) Walter Lee's twenty-year-old sister, Beneatha, is a medical student who has developed her own tough intellectual "crust." She is too immersed in her own plans and fantasies to understand or tend to the sore festering in her family. Even Travis, Ruth and Walter Lee's son, suffers: The ten-year-old's living-room bed is too public to allow him to get sufficient sleep for a growing boy.

In *A Raisin in the Sun,* the dream is not once but twice deferred. Indeed, as the play commences, the dream is not only being renewed but is tantalizingly close to becoming reality. A check for ten thousand dollars, the payment from Mr. Younger's life-insurance policy, is about to come into Mama's hands. Everyone in the family agrees that it is Mama's money to do with as she wishes, but each person, and Walter Lee especially, has his not-so-secret dreams of how to spend this sudden wealth. As we witness episodes during one month in the Younger household, we see the dreams revealed, suspended, destroyed, and renewed again. In the end, the Youngers will move into a new house that is the fulfillment of one fantasy and the beginning of others at the expense of many dreams deferred, and others blurred. . . .

## RAISIN AS A POLITICAL TOOL

Hansberry writes to persuade a white audience to accept racial integration. The strategy Hansberry uses to effect her intention is exceptionally accessible to both reader and spectators. From the play's first lines through its last, Hansberry leads the audience to feel at home with the theatrical manner of *A Raisin in the Sun* and the world it presents. The realistic setting, characters, and dialogue of *A Raisin in the Sun,* bound to a linear plot that fixes the audience's attention by presenting a problem and withholding its solution until the last scene, are for a white audience comfortably similar to the modes of American drama anthologized in paperbacks and seen yearly on Broadway. *A Raisin in the Sun* appears to be [American playwrights Eugene] O'Neill without heavy symbols, [Arthur] Miller without allegory, [Tennessee] Williams without flashbacks; from the moment the curtain rises on the customary box set, the audience feels reassured that this play will not assault its sensibilities or make disturbing demands on its relation to the stage.

Equally central to Hansberry's strategy, the specific characteristics of the people on stage and the problems they confront are recognizable and familiar. There is, of course, for white spectators one essential difference in the characters before them: They are all black. But this is, simply, the point. No spectator can ignore the blackness of the people onstage, but the white spectator is also led to perceive how much these people are like him and his family. The audience is drawn into the family onstage by the presentation in Act I of incidents so like those we are accustomed to in our own families, be they black or white, that we come to feel kinship with the stage family. Hansberry impresses us so consistently with our similarities to the people on stage that when, in Act II, a strange white man who is in no way connected to the family enters the room, he is an intruder to white spectators as well as to black spectators and those onstage.

Nor does Hansberry rest with showing likenesses. The black characters onstage not only arouse empathy through the ordinariness of their problems and behaviors, they are often admirable and, more frequently, witty and funny. The Youngers relieve anxieties in white spectators and reaffirm self-respect in black spectators, but they also delight and interest their entire audience. *A Raisin in the Sun* resists classification as a comedy or farce because of its persistently somber undertone and the frequent proximity of events to tragic resolution, but Hansberry does skillfully and consistently use humor as a kind of insurance for the success of her intention: The laughter that the dialogue incites is more frequently with the Youngers than at them. That laughter insures that we will like these people, that we will find their presence before us pleasing. If the white audience can find the Youngers pleasing in the theater, they may then accept them in their neighborhoods and schools. Each moment of the play not only amuses us or holds us in suspense, it also provides a stone that when laid beside or above all the others, will seem to make a firm wall for a house we can imagine inhabiting. . . .

## WALTER'S REDEMPTION

Our attention is all on Walter as the final portion of the play begins. Walter has "set this scene," and the other Youngers, like the audience, are witnesses. Lindner, the white man from the neighborhood committee, returns to the Youngers' home expecting, as we do, that Walter is about to sell the house to the white community. Just as Hansberry has played with our curiosity in previously unpredictable scenes with Lindner and then Bobo, she now elongates Walter's response to Lindner. In words that approach a parody of Lindner's earlier speech, while sustaining an air of utter sincerity, Walter speaks slowly of his family, of his pride in his sister's studies, and with increasing emphasis, of his father. Our attention is held rapt because this is not the role Walter has rehearsed; we have no reason not to expect him eventually to come to his deal, but the words he speaks suggest a sentiment and pride we have not seen previously in Walter. We are thus only vaguely prepared for Walter's sudden reversal. Crying unashamedly in front of "the man" Walter finally says that the Youngers will move into their new house, "because my father—my father—he earned it."

With these words, Walter pays a debt both to his parents and to the audience. The time and trust they and we have invested in him are now rewarded. He is behaving with the dignity we have had only glimpses of since the beginning of the play. As he continues to speak, he affirms this trust for both black and white spectators: "We don't want to make no trouble for nobody or fight no causes—but we will try to be good neighbors." Hansberry thus reassures white spectators that the Youngers do not want to cause difficulties and reassures black spectators that the Youngers will *try* to be good neighbors but will not guarantee any particular kind of behavior.

If we contemplate Walter's sudden redemption, we will be puzzled by it. The only possible motivation we are given for Walter's change of mind is the brief appearance of Travis before Lindner's arrival. Perhaps we are to infer that the sight of his son jars Walter into understanding that it is not only he who will suffer humiliation and loss of a dream. But the script does not guide the audience to that conclusion. Rather, we are given no pause to search for an explanation of Walter's new behavior. The moment Lindner leaves, Ruth cries, "LET'S GET THE HELL OUT OF HERE!" The women become so hastily involved in other activities and conversations that they suggest that Walter's redemption is too fragile and too fortunate to be questioned. The bustle of activity at the end of the play prevents excessive sentimentality, but it also demands that the audience feel satisfaction without understanding.

If we look closer at that feeling of satisfaction, we will find in it the essence of Hansberry's strategy. We are pleased that Walter has behaved with dignity and relieved that the Youngers will go on, not in futile desperation but with a sense of a new world before them. They have not changed very much, nor did Hansberry lead the audience to demand or expect great changes. The conclusion of *A Raisin in the Sun* returns us to a world of buoyant wit, and our ability once again to share laughter with the Youngers reassures us of a shared vision of the world.

## A HAPPY ENDING?

It is this very laughter, however, that prevents many spectators from perceiving the contradictions of the Youngers' world. Early in the play, our laughter relieves us from fully confronting the evidence that *A Raisin in the Sun* presents not simply the dreams of the characters but the complexities of "dreams deferred." Nor does the conclusion of the play make us ashamed of our good humor. The Youngers are back in high spirits. We can leave the theater happily persuaded that still another family has rightfully joined the infinitely extensive American middle class. . . .

The Youngers are not moving into the middle class when they move into their new house; they are simply and only moving into a house. For many Americans, the act of purchasing one's own house clearly signifies upward mobility and membership in the middle class. This signification occurs for at least two different reasons: In order to buy a house, the purchaser must present some assurances of stable income and occupation, and the act itself is one of choice. Since the dramatic structure of *A Raisin in the Sun* can exist only because a choice does exist, we can allow ourselves to believe that we are in the world of the middle class. But choice for the Youngers is poignantly and emphatically a singular event. They are only able to make a choice because the ten thousand dollar benefit from Mr. Younger's life insurance policy has suddenly appeared in their mailbox. Ironically, it is through death, not the nature of their lives, that they are able to choose to buy a house.

It is made amply clear that Hansberry cannot lie about the limitations of this move for the Youngers. Ruth recognizes fully that she will have to work herself to the bone to help keep up the mortgage payment, yet the early scenes of the play remind us that she cannot continue her pregnancy in health and harmony with her domestic work. And what will happen when Ruth does have a baby? If the implied assumption is that Mama will take over the rearing of another Younger child, this must also be an assumption of further internal destruction in the family, since the tensions caused by Mama's meddling in Travis's upbringing have been poignantly demonstrated. Walter Lee's situation is at least equally closed. Not only are there no new options for him to change his occupation, for him to find work less servile than that of a chauffeur, but the dream of going into business for himself has itself been muddied. The theft of his share of the insurance policy concretely removes his chance for starting a liquor business now, but it also suggests that ventures into the world of private business necessitate a kind of cunning, distrust, and encounter with corruption that calls the entire operation into question.

To turn to Beneatha or Travis only further reveals the imprisonment of the family. Beneatha may be able at the end of the play to return to her fantasies of getting married and going off to practice medicine in Africa, but the audience, at least, should remember that such notions are now even more fantastic than before, because Walter Lee has lost not only the money for his business but Beneatha's money for school. Travis may now have a room of his own, at least until the arrival of the new baby, but how will the family find the fifty cents (if it is only fifty cents out in the white suburbs) for school activities when there is no new income and the pressures of taking care of the house will create even greater financial burdens? If Travis's own parents did not like the image of their son picking up extra money by carrying bags at the supermarket, how will the new white middle-class neighbors respond to the black boy who totes packages for a few pennies after school? The bustle of moving may allow all members of the family to repress momentarily their fears and despair, but Beneatha's earlier words to Asagai, her

African friend, are the only authentic description of where the family really finds itself: "Don't you see there isn't any real progress, Asagai, there is only one large circle that we march in, around and around, each of us our own little picture—in front of us—our own little mirage which we think is the future."

Hansberry has succeeded in persuading the audience to the legitimacy of the Youngers' aspirations, but she has simultaneously shown the extreme difficulty, if not impossibility, for this family of fulfilling their dreams of change, stability, and comfort. Hansberry directly undercuts the central middle-class American notion of "equality of opportunity" by presenting the white man, Mr. Lindner, who finally believes that opportunities for blacks should not be identical with those for whites, that blacks should not move into a white neighborhood; this is only one direct instance, however, of the limitations of opportunity for the Youngers. Mr. Lindner slams a door on the Youngers that may have appeared to have been open; other doors for the Youngers simply remain closed.

# The Younger Family
# *Is* Black America

Julius Lester

Julius Lester is a writer of books for both young
people and adults, and he is a songwriter and singer
as well. He takes issue with critics of Hansberry,
such as Nelson Algren, who claims *Raisin* is about
integration, about black people becoming part of the
white middle class. Algren and others emphasize
that underneath their black skin, the Youngers are
just like white people, which is why the white audience can love them. To the contrary, says Lester,
"Within one apartment, Lorraine Hansberry capsulized so much of black life on a myriad of levels."
Walter is typical of many African American men,
castrated by the system, and blaming it on the
women in his life. But Walter comes to recognize the
dignity in refusing to be manipulated and defined by
someone else. In this he is a hero in the manner of
Rosa Parks, who refused to give up her seat on a segregated bus to a white person in Montgomery, Alabama, in 1955. She acted not to integrate the bus or
to be just like white people, but to maintain her own
integrity in a system of cruel injustice.

The play concerns itself with the Younger family: Mama
Younger, who has survived and won; her son, Walter, the
pivotal character of the play, the black male castrated by the
blade of the American dream but who blames the castration
on his wife; Ruth, Walter's wife, who sees the wound and is
unable to stanch the bleeding and, like her Biblical name-
sake, can say, "Whither thou goest, I will go"—but Walter
will not lead; Beneatha, Walter's sister, a college student, a
black militant in a day before there was a name for her; and,
Joseph Asagai, an African student, with a vision of a black-

Excerpted from Julius Lester, Introduction to *Les Blancs: The Collected Last Plays of
Lorraine Hansberry* (New York: Random House, 1972). Reprinted by permission of the
author.

ruled Africa. Within one apartment, Lorraine Hansberry capsulized so much of black life on a myriad of levels. Here is the black male–black female conflict presented in all its painful rawness in Walter and Ruth; and here too is a history of black women, all of them beautiful in totally different ways, all of them strong in totally different ways.

Because the play ends with the Youngers moving into an all-white neighborhood, it is too easy to think that it is about integration and entering the middle class. Nelson Algren wrote that the play was about

> . . . the aspiration of the new, rising Negro mercantile class to own color TV, refrigerators that have two doors, sports cars, split-level homes, central heating, self-wiping dishes and air-conditioning. In short, it is not a play about human dignity, but how to invest wisely. . . . Dramatically, RAISIN does for the Negro people what hair straightener and skin-lightener have done for the Negro cosmetics trade. . . . As a social study, it is a good drama about real estate.

One would have expected a little more acumen from Mr. Algren.

The dramatic action involves what the Younger family will do with the ten thousand dollars insurance money from Mr. Younger's death. Mama Younger wants to buy a house and move her family out of their South Side Chicago tenement. Walter Lee wants to invest it in a liquor store. What is at stake here is not moving into a white neighborhood, as some would have it, nor is it the aspiration "to own color TV," as Mr. Algren would have it. What is at stake is the kind of human being Walter Lee Younger should be.

Walter is a typical black male of working-class parents. He has grown up in the ghetto, seen his parents work hard at menial jobs all their lives. He has married, has a son, works as a chauffeur; and his wife works as a maid. And he wants more. He sees the affluence of America around him every day. He comes into contact with it on his job and every time he goes downtown and sees white people in fine restaurants. America has defined life in material terms and Walter accepts the definition without question and, in an eloquent speech, he describes vividly the kind of life he wants. It is the American dream.

> . . . one day when you 'bout seventeen years old, I'll come home and I'll be pretty tired, you know what I mean, after a day of conferences and secretaries getting things wrong the way they do . . . 'cause an executive's life is hell, man. . . And I'll pull the car up on the driveway . . . just a plain black

Chrysler, I think, with white walls—no—black tires. More elegant. Rich people don't have to be flashy . . . though I'll have to get something a little sportier for Ruth—maybe a Cadillac convertible to do her shopping in . . . And I'll come up the steps to the house and the gardener will be clipping away at the hedges and he'll say, "Good evening, Mr. Younger." And I'll say, "Hello, Jefferson, how are you this evening?" And I'll go inside and Ruth will come downstairs and meet me at the door and we'll kiss each other and she'll take my arm and we'll go up to your room to see you sitting on the floor with catalogues of all the great schools in America around you . . . All the great schools in the world! And—and I'll say, all right son—it's your seventeenth birthday, what is it you've decided? . . . Just tell me where you want to go to school and you'll go. Just tell me, what it is you want to be—and you'll *be* it . . . Whatever you want to be—Yessir! You just name it, son . . . And I hand you the world.

Walter has been taught that he should want the world, but because he is black he has been denied the possibility of ever having it. And that only makes the pain of the desire that much more hurting. As Paolo and Francesca are blown close to each other but never allowed to touch in Dante's *Inferno,* so Walter is allowed to see what America has to offer. It is held tantalizingly before him but, always, it is just out of reach.

Sometimes, it's like I can see the future stretched out in front of me—just as plain as day. The future, Mama. Hanging over there at the edge of my days. Just waiting for me—a big, looming blank space—full of *nothing.* Just waiting for *me.* Mama—sometimes when I'm downtown and I pass them cool, quiet-looking restaurants where them white boys are sitting back and talking 'bout things . . . sitting there turning deals worth millions of dollars . . . sometimes I see guys don't look much older than me.

But Mama Younger has not let America define her. She has defined herself. And she asks him: "Son—how come you talk so much 'bout money?"

WALTER: Because it is life, Mama!

MAMA:   Oh. So now it's life. Money is life. Once upon a time freedom used to be life—now it's money. I guess the world really do change.

WALTER: No—it was always money, Mama. We just didn't know about it.

MAMA:   No . . . something has happened. You something new, boy. In my time we was worried about not being lynched and getting to the North if we could and

> how to stay alive and still have a pinch of dignity,
> too . . . Now here come you and Beneatha—talking
> 'bout things we ain't never even thought about
> hardly, me and your daddy. You ain't satisfied or
> proud of nothing we done. I mean that you had a
> home; that we kept you out of trouble till you was
> grown; that you don't have to ride to work on the
> back of nobody's streetcar. You my children—but
> how different we done become.

And it is this difference in values that the play is about.
Perhaps that would be clearer if Lorraine Hansberry had not
chosen to write about material needs and aspirations so
concretely. *A Raisin in the Sun* is no intellectual abstraction
about upward mobility and conspicuous consumption. It
goes right to the core of practically every black family in the
ghettos of Chicago, New York, Los Angeles and elsewhere.
Whether they have a picture of Jesus, Martin Luther King, or
Malcolm X on the lead-painted walls of their rat-infested
tenement, all of them want to get the hell out of there as
quickly as they can. Maybe black militants don't know it, or
don't want to admit it, but Malcolm X made a down payment
on a house in a suburban community a few weeks before he
was murdered. And one surely can't accuse Malcolm of
bourgeois aspirations. He merely wanted what every black
wants—a home of his own adequate to his needs, at a mini-
mum, and the fulfillment of his desires, at the most. Contrary to Mr. Algren's interpretation, *A Raisin in the Sun* is
most definitely about "human dignity" because Lorraine
Hansberry is concerned with the attitude we must have toward material things if we are to be their master and not
their slave. Is that attitude to be Mama's? Or is it to be Walter's? And, for blacks, locked out from these things for so
long, the question is a crucial one. As blacks acquire more
and more of America's material offerings, are they, too, going
to be transformed by their acquisitions into mindless con-
sumers like the majority of whites? Or are they going to continue to walk in the path of righteousness like their forebears? Lorraine Hansberry summarized it well when, in a
letter, she wrote of the play:

> . . . we cannot . . . very well succumb to monetary values and
> know the survival of certain interior aspects of man which . . .
> must remain if we are to loom larger than other creatures on
> this planet. . . . Our people fight daily and magnificently for a
> more comfortable material base for their lives; they desper-
> ately need and hourly sacrifice for clean homes, decent food,

personal and group dignity and the abolition of terroristic violence as their children's heritage. So, in that sense, I am certainly a materialist in the first order.

However, the distortion of this aspiration surrounds us in the form of an almost maniacal lusting for "acquisitions." It seems to have absorbed the national mentality and Negroes, to be sure, have certainly been affected by it. The young man in the play, Walter Lee, is meant to symbolize their number.

Consequently, in the beginning, he dreams not so much of being comfortable and imparting the most meaningful gifts to his son (education in depth, humanist values, a worship of dignity) but merely of being what it seems to him the "successful" portion of humankind is—"rich." Toward this end he is willing to make an old trade; urgently willing. On the fact that some aspect of his society has brought him to this point, the core of the drama hangs.

Walter blames himself, his wife and his mother for what he sees as his personal failure. And only at the end of the play does it become possible for him to realize that there is a puppeteer manipulating him, a puppeteer who brought him dangerously close to destroying his family and himself.

The climax of the play comes after Walter's deal to get a liquor license falls through. Mama Younger has made a $3500 down payment on a house and gives the remaining money to Walter to do with as he wishes after he deposits $2500 in a savings account for Beneatha's education. Walter, however, takes the entire $6500 and gives it to one of his two future "partners." One of the "partners" absconds with the money. A Mr. Lindner, a white man from the neighborhood into which they are to move, comes and offers to buy the house from them for more than they would eventually pay. The whites in the neighborhood do not want a black family moving in. Previously, Walter had scornfully turned the man down. However, when he learns that his money has been stolen, he calls Mr. Lindner on the phone and tells him that they will sell the house. Mr. Lindner comes over and Walter finds that be is unable to go through with it. There is something in him—a little bit of self-respect is still left; he tells Mr. Lindner that they are going to move in. And with Walter making his first step toward being a man, a *black* man, the play ends.

Few see the heroism in Walter's simple act of assertion. Indeed, how many who have seen the play or the movie have not thought that Walter was a fool for *not* accepting the money? How one views Walter's act is a direct reflection of how much one accepts the American dream. And there is the significance of the fact that the play ends with the Youngers moving into a "white" neighborhood. To see this as a confirmation of the American dream is to accept the myth that blacks have wanted nothing more than to be integrated with whites. In actuality, the fact that the neighborhood is white is the least important thing about it. It merely happened to be the neighborhood in which Mama Younger could find a nice house she could afford. And it is this simple, practical element which has always been mistaken by whites as a desire on the part of blacks to be "integrated." But why, the question could be raised, would the Youngers persist in moving into a neighborhood where they are not wanted, where they may be subjected to harassment or even physical violence? They persist, as all blacks persist, not because it is any great honor to live among whites, but because one cannot consider himself a human being as long as he acquiesces to restrictions placed upon him by others, particularly if those restrictions are based solely on race or religion. If Walter had accepted the money, he would have been saying, in graphic language, You are right, we are niggers and don't have the right to live where we can afford to. But, with that earthy eloquence of a black still close to his roots, Walter says, "We have decided to move into our house because my father—my father—he earned it." And, in that realization, Walter learns also that it was not a black woman who castrated him. It was America and his own acceptance of America's values. No woman can make him a man. He has to do it himself.

He is a hero, a twentieth-century hero. We still long, of course, for the heroes who seemed to ride history as if it were a bronco and they were champion rodeo riders. But those heroes—if they were ever real—come from a time when life, perhaps, was somewhat less complex. But the problems that face man in the latter twentieth century are large, larger than any one of us, and the sword of a knight in armor is laughable to the dragons roaming our countryside. Our heroes are more difficult to recognize only because they appear so small beside the overwhelming enemies they must slay. But because they appear small does not mean that they are, and it does not make their acts less heroic. Walter Lee Younger has his contemporary historic counterpart in the person of a small, quiet black woman named Rosa Parks who refused to get out of a seat on a bus in Montgomery, Alabama. It would have been so easy for her to have relinquished her seat to a white person that day—as it would have been easy for Walter to have taken the money. But something in her, as in him, said No. And in that quiet dissent, both of them said Yes to human dignity. They said No to those who would define them and thereby deny their existence, and by saying No, they began to define themselves. There have been many Rosa Parks, but few of them have mysteriously set in motion a whole movement for social change. Walter Lee Younger is one of those whose act probably set nothing in motion. And that only increases its heroic dimension. In an article in *The Village Voice,* which compared Walter to Willie Loman, Lorraine Hansberry described the hero she saw in Walter Younger:

> For if there are no waving flags and marching songs at the barricades as Walter marches out with his little battalion, it is not because the battle lacks nobility. On the contrary, he has picked up in his way, still imperfect and wobbly in his small view of human destiny, what I believe Arthur Miller once called "the golden thread of history." He becomes, in spite of those who are too intrigued with despair and hatred of man to see it, King Oedipus refusing to tear out his eyes, but attacking the Oracle instead. He is that last Jewish patriot manning his rifle in the burning ghetto at Warsaw; he is that young girl who swam into sharks to save a friend a few weeks ago; he is Anne Frank, still believing in people; he is the nine small heroes of Little Rock; he is Michelangelo creating David, and Beethoven bursting forth with the Ninth Symphony. He is all those things because he has finally reached out in his tiny moment and caught that sweet essence which is human dignity, and it shines like the old star-touched dream that is in his eyes.

Part of the unrecognized genius of Lorraine Hansberry was a compassion for people that allowed her to see that there is no difference between Michelangelo, Beethoven, Oedipus and a black chauffeur on the South Side of Chicago. To our minds, besotted with self-righteous intellectuality, her comparisons are absurd and ludicrous. But heroes abound in our society—the teacher who endures the soul-killing bureaucracy of boards of education because he/she loves the children who enter the room each morning; the lunch-counter waitress who cares that your fifteen or twenty minutes at lunch are good ones; the cab driver who wants each passenger to leave his cab feeling a little better than when he entered. The heroes are with us; we simply have to learn to recognize them.

As a dramatist, Lorraine Hansberry had the gift of making us see the extraordinary in those who society had decreed were merely ordinary. The Younger family *is* black America, and the way she handles them as a dramatist is a good example of Mama Younger's advice in the play to her daughter:

> When you starts measuring somebody, measure him *right*, child, measure him right. Make sure you done taken into account what hills and valleys be come through before he got to wherever he is. . . .

Lorraine Hansberry "measures" all of her characters "right," even Mr. Lindner, of whom she once wrote in a letter:

> I have treated him as a human being merely because he is one; that does not make the meaning of his call less malignant, less sick. All that he stands for in his meandering, uncertain and polluted quest for "a way out" is detrimental to the best interests of the future of this nation and of the human race.

In the play he is not a caricature, but a person and we see and experience him for who he is. Lorraine Hansberry was an artist, not a preacher—which too many seem to think is the principal role the black artist should play today. She did not simplify the complexities of human beings, whether she agreed with them politically or not. Lesser artists are so concerned with communicating their "message" that their characters never get off the ventriloquist's knee. Lorraine Hansberry always had a message; she wouldn't have been a writer if she hadn't. But she was aware that "whatever is said must be said through the living arguments of human beings in conflict with other human beings, with themselves, with the abstractions which seem to them to be 'their society.'"

The Younger family is one particular black family living in a very particular place. And because she draws them with such precise fidelity, they are true to the social, cultural and political environment in which they live and, by being so, they become universal—as Leopold and Molly Bloom become universal. Yet Lorraine Hansberry quite rightly resented those whites who, in grasping the universality of the play, wanted to diminish the significance of the black particulars.

People are trying to say ... that this is not what they consider the traditional treatment of the Negro in the theatre. They're trying to say that it isn't a propaganda play, that it isn't something that hits you over the head; they are trying to say that they believe the characters in our play transcend category. However, it is an unfortunate way to try and say it, because I believe that one of the most sound ideas in dramatic writing is that in order to create the universal, you must pay very great attention to the specific. Universality, I think, emerges from the truthful identity of what is.

In other words, I have told people that not only is this a Negro family, specifically and definitely culturally, but it's not even a New York family or a southern Negro family. It is specifically Southside Chicago ... that kind of care, that kind of attention to detail. In other words, I think people, to the extent we accept them and believe them as who they're supposed to be, to that extent they can become everybody. So I would say it is definitely a Negro play before it is anything else.

To try and deny that *Raisin* is a black play is to deny the very particular ways in which blacks express their humanity (and what is culture if it is not a particular expression of humanity?).

# CHAPTER 2

# The Female Aspect of the Play

READINGS ON
A RAISIN IN THE SUN

# Debunking the Myth of the Emasculating Woman

Sharon Friedman

Sharon Friedman's selection is based on her New York University doctoral dissertation entitled *Feminist Concerns in the Works of Four Women Dramatists.* She writes that *Raisin* disputes the claim by black men that their women do not do enough to support them in their efforts to rise from poverty and white oppression, to "be somebody."

Hansberry portrays with compassion the plight of a woman like Ruth, who strives to bolster the male ego of a husband battered by racism and poverty while at the same time dealing with her own experience of racism and poverty.

One of the least recognized aspects of Hansberry's plays are the feminist concerns woven into her exploration of racial and economic oppression, and the struggle against political and human alienation. Writing on the eve of the recent feminist resurgence, Hansberry anticipates in her characterizations of strong and admirable black women the black feminists of the '60s and '70s who have repudiated attacks upon black women, particularly mothers, as castrating and conservative—a restraining force upon rebellion. Hansberry's mothers are at times difficult, but they are also supportive and often revolutionary.

In an article titled "This Complex of Womanhood," Hansberry's most direct feminist statement, she brings attention to the realities underlying stereotypical images of black women:

> . . . On the one hand . . . she is saluted as a monument of endurance and fortitude, and in whose bosom all comforts reside . . . and, at the same time, another legend of the Negro

Excerpted from Sharon Friedman, "Feminism as Theme in Twentieth-Century American Women's Drama," *American Studies,* vol. 25 (1984), pp. 84–85. Reprinted with permission.

woman describes the most . . . deprecating creature ever placed on earth to plague . . . the male. She is seen as an over-practical, unreasonable source of the destruction of all vision and totally lacking a sense of the proper "place" of woman-hood.

Either image taken alone is romance; put together they em-brace some truths and present the complex of womanhood which . . . now awakens to find itself inextricably . . . bound to the world's most insurgent elements. . . . [in] the United States, a seamstress refuses one day, simply refuses, to move from her chosen place on a bus while an equally remarkable sister of hers ushers children past bayonets in Little Rock. It is indeed a single march, a unified destiny, and the prize is the future. . . . In behalf of an ailing world which surely needs our defiance, may we, as Negroes or *women* never accept the notion of "our place."

In *A Raisin in the Sun* (1959), Hansberry's drama about a family anxious to leave their roach-infested apartment on Chicago's Southside, she portrays such a traditional and at the same time forward looking woman in the character of Lena Younger. Lena or Mama, as she is called, comes into conflict with her son Walter about the means for attaining a better life for their family—his sister, wife and child. The play employs a device, a $10,000 insurance policy that comes to Lena after her husband's death. Lena as well as the other women want to buy a house and move the family out of the ghetto. She also plans to set money aside for her daughter's medical education. But Walter, pained by his life as a chauffeur and by his inability to provide for his family, wants to invest in a liquor store, and ultimately loses a large sum in pursuit of quick money.

## MISGUIDED ANGER TOWARD WOMEN

Walter eventually attains a sense of self-realization, not by forfeiting his dreams and acquiescing to the women's de-mands, nor by moving into a white neighborhood, but rather by resisting the attempts of the white community to exclude him by buying him off. Moreover, Walter's self-awareness is achieved through transferring the target of his resentment from black women to those who have the power to control his fate.

Early in the play, Walter castigates black women (his wife Ruth in particular) for not "building their men up and mak-ing 'em feel like they somebody. Like they can do some-thing. . . ." Because black women exert a profound influence

## THE MOTHER-DAUGHTER BOND

*The power of shared femaleness makes the mother-daughter relationship especially significant, according to Ellen Handler Spitz, author of* Art and Psyche: A Study in Psychoanalysis, Museums of the Mind, *and* Image and Insight. *Tracing this powerful bond to the ancient myths, she finds it clearly exemplified in* Raisin*'s Lena and Beneatha.*

In order to focus on the mother-daughter dyad, the myth . . . relegates its male characters to the periphery. . . .

The death of Lena's husband occurs before any action takes place in Lorraine Hansberry's play, "A Raisin in the Sun," which is dedicated "To Mama: in gratitude for the dream." The absence of the husband and father here leaves the stage open at the end of Scene One for a uniquely powerful moment in American theater: Beneatha, fiercely independent, headstrong, and twenty, having just treated her mother to a barrage of typical adolescent jargon on her inalienable right to express herself, culminates with the statement: "God is just one idea I don't accept."

The ensuing stage directions read:

> (MAMA absorbs this speech, studies her daughter and rises slowly and crosses to Beneatha and slaps her powerfully across the face. After, there is only silence and the daughter drops her eyes from her mother's face, and Mama is very tall before her.)
>
> MAMA Now—you say after me, in my mother's house there is still God. . . . *In my mother's house* there is still God.

Well-acted, this scene conveys the sheer weight of ongoing maternal presence as it shapes the consciousness of a daughter. With keen insight, Lorraine Hansberry crafts Lena's contrasting behavior towards Beneatha and towards her son Walter Lee. Innately in tune with the headstrong young pre-med student who is obviously a second edition of herself, Lena readily guides, disciplines, supports *and opposes* her; she knows she can count on Beneatha's strength, just as she can count on her own. With Walter Lee, on the other hand, her interventions falter and misfire, and she comes only painfully, and after loss, to a rapprochement with him. . . .

[We] recognize the power of *gendered sameness* and of biology—to see, in other words, that, because the girl *is* a second edition of her mother, their object relations are deeply structured by this sameness.

Ellen Handler Spitz, "Mothers and Daughters: Ancient and Modern Myths," *Journal of Aesthetics and Art Criticism* (Fall 1990), pp. 415–16.

on family decisions, they are seen to be a further assault on his manhood. Walter perceives their strength as a source of his weakness.

Hansberry rejects the idea that black women "emasculate" black men, as well as the notion that emasculation is the cause of black social and economic inferiority. *A Raisin in the Sun* debunks these myths by portraying the real causes of frustration and self-hatred: the race prejudice and economic exploitation which oppress black men and women alike, and which strain their personal relations.

Hansberry's feminism is implicit in her dramatization of these personal relations within the domestic sphere. The condition of women forced to work at subsistence wages and relegated to domestic labor is epitomized by Hansberry in her portrayal of the black domestic who must clean the kitchens of white women as well as her own. At the same time, she is expected to bolster the male ego which has been deflated by racism and poverty. Because it is women who are charged with the responsibility of raising children and maintaining the home even under the most adverse conditions, it is not surprising that Hansberry portrays the women in this play as particularly anxious to acquire a better home. Yet because of their urgency to move the family out of the ghetto, they are vulnerable to Walter's accusations (shared by some critics) of "not thinking big enough" and of frustrating men's ambitions. Hansberry's answer is that the ghetto kills, not only the dreams to which Mama clings, but the bodies of the children Ruth must feed or abort.

# Teachers of Manly Dignity and Pride

Anthony Barthelemy

*Raisin*'s women demonstrate strength and determination in the character of Ruth, a trailblazing spirit in the character of Beneatha, and above all, dignity and pride in the character of Lena. Anthony Barthelemy, author of *Miserable Fortune: The Representation of Blacks in English Drama, 1589–1695*, writes that in the absence of strong male characters in the play, Walter must learn these manly qualities from the women who possess them, especially his mother.

We must finally recognize that Hansberry wrote *A Raisin in the Sun* with a feminist commitment and her portrayal of black women is politically charged.

Just two days before the first performance of *A Raisin in the Sun* in New Haven, Hansberry wrote her mother:

> Mama, it is a play that tells the truth about people, Negroes and life and I think it will help a lot of people to understand how we are just as complicated as they are—and just as mixed up—but above all, that we have among our miserable and downtrodden ranks—people who are the very essence of human dignity. That is what, after all the laughter and tears, the play is supposed to say. I hope it will make you very proud.

That Hansberry sought to affirm the dignity of black people and to make her mother proud—she dedicates the play "To Mama: in gratitude for the dream"—goes far to explain Lena Younger, Mama of *A Raisin in the Sun*. In her mother, Hansberry found a real life example of the strong black woman who fights and endures for her family. In a letter to the New York *Times* in April 1964, Hansberry recalls a remarkable episode concerning her mother, an episode that surely helped to shape Lena and the action of *A Raisin in the Sun*.

Excerpted from Anthony Barthelemy, "Mother, Sister, Wife: A Dramatic Perspective," *Southern Review*, vol. 21, no. 3 (1985), pp. 773–79. Reprinted by permission of the author.

After the Hansberrys moved into their home in a "hellishly hostile white neighborhood," her mother literally armed herself to protect her family from "howling mobs." "And I also remember," she writes, "my desperate and courageous mother, patrolling our house all night with a loaded German luger, doggedly guarding her four children, while my father fought the respectable part of the battle in the Washington Court.". . .

Lena demands of her children respect and dignity, and in return she gives them love and understanding. . . . Hansberry's Lena represents the proud norm, the woman who takes in ironing, cleans white folks' houses and who never ceases to boast: "I come from five generations of people who was slaves and sharecroppers—but ain't nobody in my family never let nobody pay 'em no money that was a way of telling us we wasn't fit to walk the earth. We ain't never been that poor. We ain't never been that dead inside."

In the 1920 essay "The Damnation of Women," [black scholar and activist] W.E.B. Du Bois wrote:

> So some few women are born free, and some amid insult and scarlet letters achieve freedom; but our women in black had freedom thrust contemptuously upon them. With that freedom they are buying an untrammeled independence and dear as is the price they pay for it, it will in the end be worth every taunt and groan. Today the dreams of the mothers are coming true. We have still our poverty and degradation, our lewdness and our cruel toil; but we have, too, a vast group of women of Negro blood who for strength of character, cleanness of soul, and unselfish devotion of purpose, is today easily the peer of any group of women in the civilized world.

It is this woman . . . whom Hansberry felt compelled to restore, to place before both white and black America as the true representative of black women. . . . Lena Younger displays "the very essence of human dignity."

## RUTH'S DEDICATION TO THE FAMILY

Hansberry draws the other female characters with the same feminist intent. Ruth, the wife/mother of *A Raisin in the Sun*, is a firm but loving mother. She takes in ironing so that she can contribute to the family income. . . . Ruth never wavers in her support of or devotion to her husband. She takes his part against his mother on the subject of opening a liquor store:

MAMA: We ain't no business people, Ruth. We just plain working folks.

RUTH: Ain't nobody business people till they go into business. Walter Lee say colored people ain't never going to start getting ahead till they start gambling on some different kinds of things in the world—investments and things.

After it is learned that Walter Lee has lost the money, even Mama loses for a moment her determination and thinks it best to remain in their old, cramped and dismal apartment, but not Ruth. She knows that to save her marriage and her family they must move into the new house. She demands that the family rise to the circumstances and meet them with renewed resolve and strength:

MAMA: [I] Just aimed too high all the time—

RUTH: Lena—I'll work . . . I'll work twenty hours a day in all the kitchens in Chicago . . . I'll strap my baby on my back if I have to and scrub all the floors in America and wash all the sheets in America if I have to—but we got to move . . . we got to get out of here. . . .

Ruth's response . . . reflects the "truth" about black people and black women Hansberry sought to bring to the stage. "Black women could hardly strive for weakness," Angela Davis writes in *Women, Race and Class:* "they had to become strong for their families and their communities needed their strength to survive. Evidence of the accumulated strengths of Black women have forged through work, work and more work can be discovered in the contributions of the many outstanding female leaders who have emerged within the Black community. Harriet Tubman, Sojourner Truth, Ida Wells and Rosa Parks are not exceptional Black women as much as they are epitomes of Black womanhood." Broadway had seen many black housekeepers and chore-women, but Hansberry animated for Broadway and America the black women who struggle against the odds for husband, family and community. She created female characters in the image of Ida Wells and Harriet Tubman. After all, Hansberry knew in the most personal way one of these "epitomes of black womanhood."

## BENEATHA THE TRAILBLAZER

As Ruth embodies the strength and determination of these epitomes, her sister-in-law, Beneatha, possesses their pioneering spirit. . . . She wants to be a doctor, and although she receives abuse from her brother and her American suitor,

George Murchison, for her ambition, her mother and her Nigerian suitor, Joseph Asagai, support and encourage her. . . . Beneatha is motivated by generosity and selflessness, but how different are their paths. She wants to be a doctor because ". . . [t]hat was the most marvelous thing in the world. . . . I always thought it was the one concrete thing in the world that a human being could do. Fix up the sick, you know—and make them whole again. . . ."

To be sure, Beneatha is her brother's most harsh critic and she comes to despise him after he loses the money, including the three thousand dollars that were to be set aside for her medical education. But her mother, who knows too well the bitterness of defeat, tells her why she must love her brother even more when he is down:

> Have you cried for that boy [Walter Lee] today? I don't mean for yourself and for the family 'cause we lost the money. I mean for him; what he been through and what it done to him. Child, when do you think is the time to love somebody the most; when they done good and made things easy for everybody? Well then, you ain't through learning—because that ain't the time at all. It's when he's at his lowest and can't believe in hisself 'cause the world done whipped him so. When you starts measuring somebody, measure him right, child, measure him right. Make sure you done taken into account what hills and valleys he come through before he got to wherever he is.

Ruth already knows this; that is why she cannot allow the family to relinquish its new home, its new life and its hopes. . . .

## THE WOMEN TRIUMPH

As we see in Beneatha, Hansberry's women are not plaster saints. They confess their errors, and they learn from each other. But they are women in whom Hansberry could take pride. Lena may waver in her determination, but she does not attack her son, nor does she evidence any bigotry. Ruth may argue with her husband, but never does she turn on him. Beneatha, critic that she is, remains a fiercely proud black woman who has some growing up to do but needs no apology. From her parents, Hansberry has said, she learned that "above all, there were two things which were never to be betrayed: the family and the race." The Younger women live this ideal. . . .

In the last scene of *A Raisin in the Sun*, moving men arrive to carry the Youngers' furniture out of their rented apartment and into their newly purchased home. The movement of the furniture is an important symbol for Hansberry. As the furniture is moved out, it signifies the family's move out of the ghetto and into bourgeois America. They have taken possession of their share of the American dream. Progress is being made. . . . Though there was real trauma when Hansberry's family took possession of their new home, there was also real triumph and progress for the race. Hansberry transfers that triumph onto the stage. . . .

## WALTER'S DIGNITY LOST AND FOUND

The triumph of the Younger family is indisputably engineered by Lena. She goes out alone, finds the home and makes the down payment from her ten thousand dollar insurance check. Her son Walter Lee initially opposes her decision, and for a moment he considers accepting the bribe from the white neighborhood association not to move into the house and their all-white neighborhood. He does a chilling Uncle Tom routine to show the family how he will humiliate himself to get the money from the neighborhood association. Earlier he demonstrates questionable judgment by giving sixty-five hundred dollars to someone who swindles him. And he proves to be somewhat untrustworthy by actually stealing the three thousand dollars Lena wants set aside for Beneatha's medical education. Walter Lee's actions raise questions about Hansberry's portrayal of black men. Does she see them as weak? foolish? childish? Does Lena in her strength perform the castration of her son that William Grier and Price Cobbs attribute to black mothers in their book *Black Rage:* "The black mother shares a burden with her soul sisters of three centuries ago. She must produce and shape and mold a unique type of man. She must intuitively cut off and blunt his masculine assertiveness and aggression lest these put the boy's life in jeopardy.". . .

The play ends celebrating not just the Youngers taking possession of their new home but also Walter Lee's coming finally "into his manhood." Throughout the play there is a lament for the absence of black manhood, manhood lost when Big Walter, Lena's husband and Walter Lee's father, died. The play does not suggest that true black manhood does not exist; it is just not present in the Youngers' house. And nothing is an adequate substitute for that absence, least of all the ten thousand dollar insurance check Lena gets after Big Walter's death. "Ten thousand dollars they give you. Ten thousand dollars," Lena says as she examines the newly arrived check. Hansberry's stage directions to the actress speaking these words are significant here: "She [Lena] does not look at RUTH; her eyes seem to be seeing something somewhere very far off." It is clear that Lena would give up the ten thousand dollars for the return of her husband. It is equally clear that Big Walter presided over his family as a traditional patriarch. Although Lena confides to Ruth, ". . . there was plenty wrong with Walter Younger—hardheaded, mean, kind of wild with women," she overlooks his flaws and loves his strengths. It is the strength of his father that Lena demands from her son: "I am waiting to hear how you be your father's son." The ideal of black manhood is there; unfortunately, it goes unemulated until the last scene.

In the end, Lena commands Walter to act like the *pater familias* [male head of a household] and although there is a certain amount of irony, probably unintended, in her demand, rather than "intuitively cut off and blunt [Walter Lee's] masculine assertiveness," Lena pushes for just the opposite. When Walter finally becomes his father's son, he hands down a legacy of pride and dignity to his young son, Travis. He tells the representative of the white neighborhood association: ". . . we called you over here to tell you that we are very proud and that this is—this is my son, who makes the sixth generation of our family in this country, and that we have all thought about your offer and we have decided to move into our house because my father—my father—he earned it." When the representative looks to Lena to overrule her son—something the audience knows she would not hesitate to do if she thought him wrong—she replies: "I am afraid you don't understand. My son said we was going to move and there ain't nothing left for me to say." When Walter truly fills the role of *pater familias*, Lena abdicates with joy; she willingly retires to her garden. Now that her son has grown into a man, she can tend her "feeble little plant."

## TEACHERS OF MANHOOD

It may seem strange to say Hansberry's intentions were feminist, if at the play's end Lena seems to surrender and lovingly endorses the idea of patriarchy. But the play endorses patriarchy not at the expense of female strength or female governance. Manhood in *A Raisin in the Sun* is wholly compatible with feminism. Lena does not surrender judgment to Walter simply because he is a man; she acquiesces because Walter is right. Manhood cannot be achieved until Walter demonstrates the pride and dignity that the women already possess. Hansberry would agree with Du Bois who wrote in "The Damnation of Women": "What is today the message of these black women to America and to the world? The uplift of women is, next to the problem of the color line and the peace movement, our greatest modern cause. When, now, two of these movements—women and color—combine in one, the combination has deep meaning."

# A Feminist Perspective

Adrienne Rich

Poet, critic, and radical feminist Adrienne Rich offers a complex view of Hansberry. On one hand, Rich is frankly impressed with Hansberry's feminist credentials in her political writing and her prophetic anticipation of the issues to come, such as "the politics of housework, pornography (which she recognized immediately as a feminist issue), women's work outside the home, the politics of dress and adornment, the socialist position regarding women's role and much else that the late 1960's wave of feminism was to address as if for the first time."

But at the same time, in her plays, Hansberry ultimately has men in the heroic roles, as when the focus clearly shifts to Walter as the central character of *Raisin* over Mama, Beneatha, Ruth, or all three, as these profoundly conceived women characters are reduced to cheerleaders for a male hero. Something like this happens in Hansberry's other plays as well. Rich raises the possibility that Hansberry may have had to choose between her commitments to the liberation of African Americans and that of women, and she may have consciously or unconsciously muted her feminism to give her plays a better chance of being produced on Broadway. But Rich emphasizes that these are questions that need to be investigated by responsible scholars, preferably black feminists.

I wish to address the life/work of Lorraine Hansberry from a woman's perspective, a feminist perspective, within the limitations of my experience as a white woman. I cannot assume knowledge of what the characters Beneatha and Ruth would have meant to a young black woman student, or married woman, in 1959; what Lena Younger would have meant to an older black woman in the theatre audiences of that year. But as a feminist critic, my concern is not only to read the work of the past and present women writers with a woman-identified perspective; it is to help create more possibilities for women writers in the future. My task, therefore, is to comprehend how the political meaning of being a woman shapes and affects both substance and form in women's art; what are the interruptions, silences, resistances, censorships confronted by a woman artist working in a dominant culture which derogates both the female body and female creativity. A decade of white feminist criticism has taught us much about the circumstances under which women have written at all, much about the struggles and choices involved in getting that writing read. But within white feminist criticism itself there have been notable silences, erasures. The black woman writer, as Barbara Smith has noted, suffers from a double erasure:

> When Black women's books are dealt with at all, it is usually in the context of Black literature which largely ignores the implications of sexual politics. When white women look at Black women's works they are of course ill-equipped to deal with the subtleties of racial politics.

To read Lorraine Hansberry, to understand the meaning of her work, means for me of necessity to question all filters, all "translations"; to view the work in the context of what it means to be both black and female in a world where each is a stigmatized or erased identity. I cannot afford the luxury of an unexamined "humanism," a position defined and ordered by white males; no more can I accept any male judgment as to the intrinsic radicalism of any woman, black or white.

Lorraine Hansberry is a problem to me, then, because even as I read *A Raisin in the Sun* I am aware of the inner and outer contradictions spawned when a writer who is both black and female tries with passionate intent to make a statement which can be heard by those who are neither, and tries specifically to get that statement heard in the Broadway theatre—a theatre that is commercial and capitalist in the extreme. Of even the blandest, most digestible plays we know that other hands than the playwright's have snipped and smoothed, pried apart and reglued the original script with an eye to making back the investment, following those economics of the New York theatre, which Nemiroff himself has described. But even before that process begins, I know from my own experience as a white, lesbian, feminist writer that the first—and last—censors are interior when we are writing in the face of that judgment and culture of white males, that cultural jury which presumes to set standards, to determine whose experience counts, which themes are "universal" and which "parochial," to define the literary canon, to define "greatness" itself. I cannot attempt here to explore where or how this brilliant, ardent and very angry woman may have encountered both interior and exterior censors; but a few clues are available, and they fascinate me.

For example: According to Nemiroff's "Critical Background" to *Les Blancs*, in Hansberry's earliest notes for the play, made in 1960, she conceived of an African woman, Candace, returning to her tribal village *for her mother's funeral*—a daughter and a mother who apparently became transformed into the intellectual, Europeanized Tshembe and his father, the dead Kwi warrior. Lorraine Hansberry was a student of African history and culture long before the invention of Black Studies and was surely aware of the powerful woman-to-woman bonding in tribal societies, aware of the exercise of economic and political power by African women. But in the existing version of the play there is no African woman, only the vision of the Dancer in the sky. In September of the same year, Hansberry listed among her future projects a musical drama to be titled *The Sign in Jenny Reed's Window.* (When, why, did Candace become metamorphosed into Tshembe, Jenny Reed into Sidney Brustein?) In the same list of "proposed work" appears the note: *"The Life of Mary Wollstonecraft,* full length drama."

She was, it is clear, an early and lucid feminist. In 1957, she had begun the draft of an essay on de Beauvoir's *The Second Sex* in which she said, *"The Second Sex* may well be the most important work of this century." She assessed the reception of the book in America, the gossip surrounding de Beauvoir's personal life which substituted for serious debate on her ideas. In the course of this essay, she addressed the politics of housework, pornography (which she recognized immediately as a feminist issue), women's work outside the home, the politics of dress and adornment, the socialist position regarding women's role and much else that the late 1960's wave of feminism was to address as if for the first time. In 1961, she wrote an essay ironically entitled "In Defense of the Equality of *Men*," in which she challenged psy-

choanalytic theories of femaleness and, long before a movement for battered women existed, wrote:

> In a widely read women's magazine in a feature called "Mak-
> ing Marriage Work" the professor-analyst tackled what might
> seem to the excessively civilized a resolved question: "Should
> A Husband Strike His Wife?" Bending to enlightenment, the
> writer opined, "It is impossible to condone such behavior."
> He then went on, however, to modify that bit of radical aban-
> don by advising his readers that the "provocation" by wives
> was undoubtedly far greater than they realized. He offered
> the following directions to wives as to how best to avoid their
> partially deserved beatings: "Gauge his mood; avoid argu-
> ments; indulge his whims; help him relax; keep love alive."

In the same essay, she challenges the myth that American
women tyrannize over "the home and even the wealth of the
nation." She also quotes Susan B. Anthony and, again, takes
up the issue of pornography along with that of censorship.

Much earlier, at the age of 25, in a letter to the newly-
founded *Village Voice*, Hansberry had protested a laudatory
review of Strindberg's *Comrades* on the ground that

> the playwright clearly hated women. . . . It is probably true
> that if the play had had a reverse point of view that it might
> have been dismissed rapidly as a badly-written piece of
> "Feminist" *propaganda.* Sometimes it almost seems that only
> when propaganda is propagandizing a return to a dead and
> useless past is it profound,—"art"/avant-garde, etc. . . . there
> have been, as of yet, too many Strindbergs (in one degree or
> another) and too few Ibsens and Shaws. . . . The only answer,
> in drama, to Bertha Alberg [a Strindberg character] is Nora
> Helmer [an Ibsen character].

Did Lorraine Hansberry ever conceive of Candace or Jenny
Reed or Mary Wollstonecraft as her answer, in drama, to
Bertha Alberg? Did she think of Lena Younger in those terms?
In an address to the American Academy of Psycho-Therapists
in 1963, Hansberry, speaking to the followers of Freud, says of
the maligned and sentimentalized "black matriarch":

> It is she who, while seeming to cling to traditional restraints,
> drives the young on into the fire hoses and one day simply re-
> fuses to move to the back of the bus in Montgomery, or goes
> out and buys a house in an all-white community where her
> fourth child and second daughter will almost be killed by a
> brick thrown through the window by a shrieking racist mob.

She was thinking of her own mother, presumably, but also of
Lena Younger. Yet those unpublished and fragmentary clues
suggest a black feminist anger which is less clearly reflected by
the depiction of women in her plays. The women in *A Raisin in*

*the Sun* and *Sidney Brustein* flash at moments with this anger, but it is Lena's son, Walter Lee, who finally is given the *dramaturgic* confrontation with the envoy from the racist neighborhood. It is Hannibal, in *The Drinking Gourd*, her unproduced television play, who dares plot escape, who learns to read and is blinded for so doing. And there is no actual, flesh-and-blood African woman in *Les Blancs* as we have it.

Yet Hansberry said clearly, in an interview with Studs Terkel in 1959:

> Obviously the most oppressed of any oppressed group will be its women. . . . Obviously, since women, period, are oppressed in society, and if you've got an oppressed group, they're *twice* oppressed. So I should imagine that they react accordingly: As oppression makes people more militant . . . then *twice* militant, because they're *twice oppressed*. So that there's an assumption of leadership historically.

In light of this comment, I find the question of Lorraine Hansberry's female characters—their position in the plays—worth pondering. Could the American, largely white, theatre-going public of the 1950's and early '60's have accepted as a central character a female revolutionary, a confrontational figure, a strong black woman who was not Mama, who was, let us say, both angry and sexual, who could be seen moving into a more radical position as Walter Lee Younger and Sidney Brustein are seen moving as the play progresses? Could such a black heroine—one who was "twice militant," a leader, an Ida B. Wells or a Fannie Lou Hamer—gain exposure on the Broadway stage or television screen in 1979?

Hansberry also wrote several letters to the early lesbian publication, *The Ladder*, in 1957 on the economic and psychological pressures that impel many conscious lesbians into marriage; on the connections between anti-homosexuality and anti-feminism, and on the need for new, *feminist* ethics? I find myself wondering who were the women friends with whom she discussed *The Second Sex?* Who were the women she seems to be trying to reach in her unfinished essay on that book? In their book *Lesbian/Woman*, Del Martin and Phyllis Lyon remark, "Many Black women who had been involved in the homophile movement found themselves forced to make a choice between two 'Causes' that touched their lives so intimately. One of them wrote a play that was a hit on Broadway." What does this tell us about the possible censorship, self-imposed and external, that had to be confronted by the author of *A Raisin in the Sun?*

So many of the truths of women's lives, so much of women's writing, have come to us in fragments, over time, so that for decades their work is half-understood, and we have only clues as to their real stature. I think of Emily Dickinson, published for half a century in smoothed-out, tidied versions, her full power revealed only years after her death; of Virginia Woolf, labelled "Bloomsbury," elitist and mentally unstable, her political radicalism, class-consciousness, and lesbianism erased or veiled by her husband's editing, coming fully to light only within the last two or three years; of Zora Neale Hurston, whose life and work, despite Robert Hemenway's exhaustive biography, have yet to be examined in depth from a black female perspective, though both Alice Walker and Lorraine Bethel have begun to do this. Lorraine Hansberry, charged by critics on the one hand with having created a reactionary black "mammy" in Lena Younger, and on the other with advocating genocide against whites, deserves similar scrutiny. How ironic that she would come to be dismissed contemptuously by some as a liberal when she had written as early as 1962:

> I think, then, that Negroes must concern themselves with every single means of struggle: legal, illegal, passive, active, violent and non-violent. . . . They must harass, debate, petition, boycott, sing hymns, pray on steps—and shoot from their windows when the racists come cruising through their communities. . . . The acceptance of our condition is the only form of extremism which discredits us before our children.

And as early as 1957:

> Woman like the Negro, like the Jew, like colonial peoples, even in ignorance, is *incapable of accepting the role with harmony.* This is because it is an unnatural role. . . . The station of woman is hardly one that she would assume by choice, any more than men would. It must necessarily be imposed on her—by force. . . . A status not freely chosen or entered into by an individual or group is necessarily one of oppression and the oppressed are by their nature . . . forever in ferment and agitation against their condition and what they understand to be their oppressors. If not by overt rebellion or revolution, then in the thousand and one ways they will devise with and without consciousness to alter their conditions.

What, then, were Lorraine Hansberry's conscious and unconscious conflicts and choices when, as a black woman, she sought to write plays which stood any chance of being heard on the American stage? What did she dream of being free to write should she gain validation from the American white male establishment? What did it mean to be one of the tiny handful of black women artists who have found it possible to have their works published, performed or seen? What was the community, what was the loneliness, from within which she worked? It seems to me impossible to talk about what is presently visible of Lorraine Hansberry's writings without asking questions like these. Did she know, had she read, Zora Neale Hurston? What black women writers did she read? Had she read the white anti-racist southern writer Lillian Smith, who also wrote from a female consciousness?

And these questions flow into others for me—unanswerable questions, unprovable hypotheses, yet irresistible in this time and place. Where would Hansberry have placed herself, had she lived till now, in relation to the feminist movement of the present? How would she have responded to the poetry of June Jordan, to a black feminist manifesto such as the Combahee River Collective statement, to Alice Walker's "In Search of Our Mothers' Gardens" and *Meridian* to Audrey Lorde's *The Black Unicorn* or "Scratching the Surface"; to the music of Bernice Reagon, Mary Watkins, Linda Tillery; to Ntozake Shange's *For Colored Girls Who Have Considered Suicide. . .*? What would she have made of Barbara Smith's declaration that "I want most of all for Black women and Black lesbians somehow not to be so alone. This . . . will require the most expansive of revolutions as well as many new words to tell us how to make this revolution real"?

I cannot presume to have answers to these questions. Lorraine Hansberry remains a problem and a challenge. I wait for the black feminist who, with free access to Hansberry's unpublished papers, can help us see her unidealized, unsimplified, in her fullest complexity, in her fullest political context. I do know that fame and economic security are not enough to enable the woman artist—black or white—to push her art and thought to their outermost limits. For that, we need community: A community whose members know our experience from the inside out because it is their own; who will support us in our efforts to depict that experience in the face of those who would either reward us for glossing over, or punish us for articulating, the extremity in which we live.

# CHAPTER 3

# Character Studies

READINGS ON
A RAISIN IN THE SUN

# Walter as Tragic Hero

J. Charles Washington

An English professor at Howard University, J. Charles Washington is a specialist in African American drama. The conflict between Lena's and Walter's outlooks on life provide the backdrop for what Washington calls "the primary meaning of the play—the tragedy of Walter's reach for the American Dream." Walter expects much from life. He dreams big, gambles big, wants to live big. His role models have taught him that he deserves no less than a complete stake in the American dream. Because Walter dreams selflessly in behalf of his family, conceiving of himself as a provider, he has heroic nobility. But unlike his conservative mother, and like the traditional tragic hero, Walter dreams recklessly. Because of his poor judgment, he fails to become the businessman who could lift his family out of poverty. Though the Youngers move to a better home in the suburbs, Walter has to sacrifice his heroic dream. Thus he is a realistic, and tragic, hero.

The dual protagonists [Walter and Lena] and the conflict centered on their differing ways of looking at the world are what give the play dramatic tension as well as intellectual and emotional appeal. In addition, this duality provides a structure that points to the primary meaning of the play—the tragedy of Walter's reach for the American Dream. The intent of this essay is to restore the proper balance between Lena and Walter by focusing on him and his mode of thinking. . . .

## LENA'S SECOND-CLASS DREAM

Lena Younger's thinking is restricted by time. Hers is the thinking of a Black woman born near the turn of the century in a racist American society, and she does not understand

Excerpted from J. Charles Washington, "*A Raisin in the Sun* Revisited," *Black American Literature Forum*, vol. 22, no. 1 (Spring 1988), pp. 112–24. Reprinted by permission of the author.

the modern ways and thinking of her children. "Something has changed," she tells Walter. "You something new, boy. In my time we was worried about not being lynched and getting to the North if we could and how to stay alive and still have a pinch of dignity too . . . Now here come you and Beneatha—talking 'bout things we ain't never even thought about hardly, me and your daddy. You ain't satisfied or proud of nothing we done. I mean that you had a home; that we kept you out of trouble till you was grown; that you don't have to ride to work on the back of nobody's streetcar—You my children—but how different we done become.". . .

Her experiences with discrimination as a young woman in the South affected her thinking. While they did not destroy her self-esteem, they did color her outlook on life, narrowing her perspective and restricting her beliefs about what a Black person could reasonably expect to achieve in American society. The only way a Black person could escape discrimination in the South of that time was to move to the North. Though it was a compromise, the action she took meant that she was a fighter who took the step that many of her generation did in order to make a meaningful change in her life. In fact, she is still a fighter, and she proves it by buying the house to bring about the change she now feels is needed for her family's welfare. As she says, "When the world gets ugly enough, a woman will do anything for her family." Her belief in this change, which is her version of the American Dream, sets her at odds with her son Walter. Like her earlier move to the North, the purchase of a suburban Chicago house reflects a compromise or acceptance of less than she deserves or is entitled to. Hers is, in short, not the true American Dream, but a second-class version of it reserved for Black Americans and other poor people. Considering all the obstacles she has had to face as a Black woman, one can hardly fault her for what she does. Nevertheless, her dream is unacceptable to Walter, who will have nothing less than the complete American Dream, since her version of it only amounts to surviving, not living in the fullest sense.

## WALTER, THE ALL-AMERICAN

Unlike his mother, Walter has managed to escape almost completely the crippling inferiority that destroys many Blacks, men in particular. In order to help determine how he managed to acquire the strength to dream his dream, one

**WALTER'S PROPHETIC VOICE**

*Actor and playwright Douglas Turner Ward sees Walter's ultimate importance as a character in the frustration and anger he feels as a black man in white America. In 1959, when* Raisin *was first produced, most white people were either unaware of or threatened by black people's anger. But in the decade to come (the 1960s), more black voices of protest would bear out Walter's prophetic significance.*

It is Walter Lee—flawed, contradictory, irascible, impulsive, furious and, most of all, desperate—who emerges as the most unique creation for his time and ours. It is his behavior throughout the play—his restless impatience, his discontent with the way things are, his acute perception of societal disparities, his fury at status inequities, his refusal to accept his "place"—which gives the play prophetic significance, for these traits are not embodied in an exceptional prototype but are the properties of an average person, a typical member of the broad black majority. Most of the 1959 audience, encountering this anger within such a prevalent type, felt threatened. He made them uneasy; he raised unsettling doubts; he was difficult to identify with. Where would all this raging frustration lead? Despite his fixation with America's pragmatism and dreams of success, he was, in his energy, an omen. That energy was soon to erupt into American reality with a vengeance.

Douglas Turner Ward, "Lorraine Hansberry and the Passion of Walter Lee," *Freedomways* (1979), p. 225.

might examine what is most American about Walter and his thinking, for it is his acceptance of American values, rather than stereotypes, myths, and untruths about Blacks, that enables him to dream and act in a typically American way. As Hansberry has stated, ". . . Walter Younger is an American more than he is anything else." Foremost is his belief in the value which holds that, in the land of opportunity, anyone can become anything he wants to be. While the play contains no explicit evidence to support this conjecture, the fact that this democratic ideal is the most cherished of those which form the American consciousness—indeed, is synonymous with the freedom that America stands for—means that Walter would be affected by it, as all Americans are. Believers in this myth let nothing stand in their way, as he does not. For him, this includes racism, which he barely considers until he is directly confronted with it in Act II, Scene 3, in the person of Carl Lindner, who tries to bribe the family in order to keep them out of his white neighborhood. Even then it has no real effect on his dream or his plans.

Another source of Walter's strength is the fact that he is male. As Lena Younger's world view and range of possibilities are restricted by her femaleness, Walter's are enlarged and enhanced by his maleness. Another source of strength lies in his belief in himself and in his ability to do what other successful Americans have done. He sincerely believes that he is cut out for better things. Near the end of Act II, Scene 2, he describes himself as "a giant—surrounded by ants! Ants who can't even understand what it is the giant is talking about." This strong faith in himself is the basis of his typically American self-reliance and rugged individualism. . . .

## WALTER'S ROLE MODELS

Walter's dream of success was nurtured by a young white man whom he saw in town and sought to emulate. He has not modeled himself after his father, whose death and sacrifice assume a meaning for him which is radically different from that which his mother has given them. His image of his father matches the old stereotype of the hard-working, long-suffering Black male who literally worked himself to death. As Lena says, "I seen . . . him . . . night after night . . . come in . . . and then look at me . . . the red showing in his eyes . . . the veins moving in his head . . . I seen him grow thin and old before he was forty . . . working and working and working like somebody's old horse . . . killing himself. . . ." There is no way Walter could forget this image, and the check becomes the symbolic representation of the senseless waste of his father's life. Other tangible signs of it are the cramped, roach-infested apartment, the shabby furniture, and the worn out rug on the floor. No matter how much he may have loved his father, it would be unthinkable to want to replicate his father's life. For this reason, the young white men his age personify for him the true American Dream, a dream he knows he is worthy of: "Mama—sometimes when I'm downtown and pass them cool, quiet-looking restaurants where them white boys are sitting back and talking 'bout things . . . sitting there turning deals worth millions of dollars . . . sometimes I see guys don't look much older than me."

The stimulation that he gets downtown from seeing the young white men is quite different from that which he gets from the Black musicians at a Southside Chicago bar called the Green Hat: "You know what I like about the Green Hat? I like this little cat they got there who blows a sax . . . He blows. He talks to me. . . . And there's this older guy who plays the piano . . . and they got a sound. . . . They got the best little combo in the world in the Green Hat . . . You can just sit there and drink and listen to them three men play and you realize that don't nothing matter worth a damn, but just being there." The former source of stimulation invites action, while the latter induces inactivity. The actions of the young white men stimulate him to hope, dream, think, even scheme. Black music, on the other hand, becomes for him a kind of drug or narcotic that lulls him into a state of listlessness which allows him to escape depression.

His reliance on white models does not mean that he hates himself or his blackness. Rather, it is a sign of his pragmatism and confirms his self-love: He believes he can do what they do and that he deserves to have what they have. That he feels himself to be in their class is seen, for example, in his words to George Murchinson, Beneatha's suitor, whose father is a rich Black businessman whom Walter has never seen or met: "Your old man is all right, man. . . . I'd like to talk to him. Listen, man, I got some plans that could turn this city upside down. I mean I think like he does. *Big*. . . . It's hard to find a man on this whole Southside who understands my kind of thinking." Central to Walter's aspirations as a businessman is the color-neutral value of the American Dream, not the particular race of the individual who attains it. Mr. Murchinson's success in business indicates that anyone of any race can attain it.

### A NOBLE DREAM AND BAD JUDGMENT

Strong, aggressive, ambitious, ruthless even, like the men he imitates, Walter reaches for the complete American Dream. It is natural that he would, for the freedom that America grants an individual holds the possibility of unlimited riches, both spiritual and economic. What Walter dreams of and aggressively pursues is the power that money brings, power being the essence of the only kind of manhood he is willing to accept. Of course, some degree of self-aggrandizement is attached to the American Dream; many of those who attain it, such as captains of industry, do become great American heroes. However, Walter's personal stake in his dream must

be balanced by the primary purpose for which he seeks it—
a radical change in his family's living conditions. This
change is much wider in scope than Lena's planned move
from their cramped apartment to a larger suburban home. It
means a wholly different and improved standard of living: a
substantial move up the socio-economic ladder, the complete abandonment of poverty, the chance to live the kind of
life most Americans dream of living. The selflessness and
nobility of this dream are what give Walter's character its
dignity and spiritual dimension. . . .

While the freedom the individual enjoys in America provides for opportunities, it does not guarantee success. Walter's dream remains only that not because of defects in the
American system but because of basic flaws in his own
character. His recognition of the responsibility for his own
fate marks him as a tragic hero.

Though in Act III he indulges in self-pity after he has lost
the money, railing about the "takers and the 'tooken'" as he
tries to escape the blame for his failure, Walter had indicated
earlier, in Act II, Scene 3, that he was aware of the danger his
plan entailed. Speaking of his plan to George Murchinson,
Walter remarks, "Invest big, gamble big, hell, lose *big* if you
have to. . . ." He knows that the possibility of failure is also a
vital part of the American success story. Though as viewers
of the play we know this too, we are nevertheless deeply affected by his failure because of the nobility of his dream and
the vigor and intensity with which he pursues it. We have
sympathy for him in spite of the fact that he bullies his wife,
ridicules his sister's dream, deceives his mother, and attempts to bribe state officials in Springfield in order to get a
liquor license for the business. Even more serious than these
defects in his character as they affect his dream, and hence
the welfare of his family, is his flaw in judgment; he considers Willy Harris a successful businessman when he is really
an untrustworthy con man.

## A DISDAIN FOR EDUCATION

In regard to the likelihood of Walter's success in business, an
even greater flaw would be his lack of knowledge of how a
business is run. This is not to say that he requires a Harvard
M.B.A., for another vital part of the American success story
is the great number of individuals lacking formal education
who with raw talent, intelligence, drive, and luck have suc-

ceeded in establishing and running their own businesses. At the same time, Walter fails to see the potential value of education. This attitude is evident in his disparaging remarks about his sister's plans to become a doctor, although they also reflect stereotypical male chauvinism regarding the careers women should or should not pursue. More clear cut is his insulting remark to George Murchinson about "colored college boys": "I see you all the time—with books tucked under your arms—going to your 'clahsses.' And for what! What the hell you learning over there? Filling up your heads—with the sociology and the psychology—but they teaching you how to be a man? How to take over and run the world? They teaching you how to run a rubber plantation or a steel mill? Naw—just to talk proper and read books and wear white shoes. . . ."

Walter has disdain for education not only because he feels it is a waste of time, but also because the sensitive, intellectual types who pursue it do not correspond to his conception of manhood. For him, the only "real" men are the powerful ones who manage America's businesses. His mistake lies not only in his false conception of manhood but also in his failure to see that some kind of education, formal or otherwise, is a necessary requirement for his goal, particularly as there is in his community no cultural basis of business ownership comparable to that in mainstream American communities through which he could learn what he needs to know about business management. Finally, while his initial contact with young white males was positive, inasmuch as they supplied him with the inspiration for his desperate attempt to escape poverty, his casual contact with them could not provide him with the hands-on experience he needed to attain his goal. Even if he had been able to acquire the business, his chances of success would have been affected by both his lack of knowledge and his lack of experience. While Walter himself is largely responsible for his negative attitude toward education, his lack of experience, over which he has no control, points out the need for positive business contacts or role models in his own Black community. . . .

## THE SCHOOL OF HARD KNOCKS

Viewers of *A Raisin in the Sun* can be moved by a tragic hero who is elevated by his growth from ignorance to knowledge, and deeply affected by a realistic hero whose transcendence involves a tremendous sacrifice—at the play's end, Walter and his family are as poor and powerless as they were before. The new house provides a "pinch of dignity" that allows them a bit more breathing and living space, but their lives are essentially unchanged. Without the greater financial rewards the business could have produced, they must all continue working at the same menial jobs in order to survive and pay for the house. In fact, they may be even worse off, since the birth of Ruth's second child will mean an extra mouth to feed. Walter and Ruth have made no substantive economic progress; their current life is a modern version of the life of Lena and Big Walter. The principal hope that Ruth and Walter have is the one Lena and Big Walter had and which people everywhere have always had—that some day in the future their children will be able to make their parents' dreams come true. . . .

This small but significant hope, as well as the characters who embody it, offers perhaps the best example of the universal materials the play abounds in, giving Hansberry's art its distinguishing mark and enduring value. Illustrating her ability to see synthesis where others could only see dichotomy, Hansberry discovered the basis of this universal hope, indeed of her faith in humanity, in the Black experience: ". . . if blackness brought pain, it was also a source of strength, renewal and inspiration, a window on the potentials of the human race. For if Negroes could survive America, then there was hope for the human race indeed."

# Beneatha's Search for Identity

Brenda F. Berrian

Brenda F. Berrian taught African studies at the University of Pittsburgh at the time this article was published in 1987. Here she discusses African Americans' emerging awareness in the 1950s of their ties to their ancestral Africa.

Berrian reveals that, through Asagai's proposal to Beneatha, Hansberry is exploring the possibility of intercultural marriage between American and African blacks. And while the idea is romantically appealing to Hansberry, she is confused about the possible pitfalls. American blacks who moved to their "homeland" of Africa, for example, frequently had as much trouble adapting to African culture as they had in assimilating into mainstream American culture. In searching for the utopian Africa they had envisioned, many had discovered that the real Africa presented them with as many social, political, and economic difficulties as the United States had. Intercultural marriages, however, presented the potential for change.

As a secondary theme, possible marriage between a Nigerian male student and an Afro-American woman appears in the incidental passages in *A Raisin in the Sun*, the primary theme of which is the determination of a lower-middle class Afro-American family to better their standing in American society by moving from the slums to the suburbs. More broadly speaking, the play is about choices, about a son's struggle to find his manhood, and about the reaffirmation of black identity. The theme of an intercultural marriage can be viewed as a testimony of self-affirmation, new freedoms and a positive step towards black identity.

Excerpted from Brenda F. Berrian, "The Afro-American–West African Marriage Question: Its Literary and Historical Contexts," in *Women in African Literature Today*, edited by Eldred Durosimi Jones (London: James Currey, 1987). Reprinted by permission of the publisher.

Joseph Asagai, the Nigerian male student in *A Raisin in the Sun,* brings a set of new ideas and values to the theme of an Afro-American who is searching for a new lease of life and a quick, easy way to beat the system. Asagai is presented as a self-assured, well-travelled and well-spoken individual who is Beneatha Younger's pathway to a completed search for her identity. Through his marriage proposal to Beneatha he offers a promise of life in a soon-to-be independent Nigeria as opposed to life in Chicago as a wife to a bourgeois Afro-American with all the dullness and pretentiousness that the latter entails.

## THE QUESTION OF ASSIMILATION

Beneatha is portrayed as a 20-year-old woman who is restless, unsettled, bored, studying to be a doctor and in search of something new, different, and alien to her environment. Asagai and his stories about Nigeria bring a breath of fresh air to an otherwise stifling, and almost intolerable situation. Beneatha's relationship with Asagai makes her aware of the desire of Afro-Americans to merge into the dominant American society. This is shown in Beneatha's conversation with her sister-in-law and her Afro-American boyfriend, George:

RUTH:         Why must you and your brother make an argument out of everything people say?

BENEATHA:   Because I hate assimilationist Negroes!

RUTH:         Will somebody tell me what assimila-who-means!

GEORGE:      Oh, it's just a college girl's way of calling people Uncle Toms—but that isn't what it means at all.

RUTH:         Well, what does it mean?

BENEATHA:   (*Cutting George off and staring at him as she replies to Ruth*): It means someone who is willing to give up his own culture and submerge himself completely in the dominant, and in this case, oppressive culture!

This conversation and an earlier one that takes place when Mama Younger asks Beneatha 'Why should I know about Africa?' illustrates the limited knowledge that most Afro-Americans have of Africa. Consequently, the popular *A Raisin in the Sun* helped to usher in a new awareness of Africa which would develop and mature among Afro-Americans from the late 1950s to the present. Some Afro-Americans represented by Mama and George who had been bombarded with false Tarzan-inspired images will not be able to make a positive identification with Africa.

## THE QUESTION OF PRIDE

Kwame Nkrumah's open invitation to Afro-Americans to come to Ghana when that country became independent in 1957, and the arrival of African representatives to the United Nations, encouraged Afro-Americans to replace their feelings of indifference, rejection, and shame for Africa with those of acceptance, pride, and appreciation. Africa became visible, an important news item, and many Afro-Americans like Hansberry's Beneatha seized the opportunity to identify in a positive way with the African continent. Eventual marriages between Africans and Afro-Americans was a most natural next step. Asagai's proposal of marriage to Beneatha comes as a surprise neither to the readers nor to the audience of the Hansberry play.

At the opposite pole Asagai's rival, George Murchison, represents 'money', for he is from a well-established Afro-American middle-class family. For Beneatha's family, George represents good husband material, for money means security and stability—something that the Youngers themselves want. They encourage Beneatha to consider George; however, he does not fit into Beneatha's current plans to find her African heritage. George, in turn, cannot understand her curiosity and even rejects being called 'Black Brother' by Beneatha's brother, Walter Younger. He considers Beneatha's African robe 'eccentric' and rejects the lecture on the 'Great West African Heritage'. George plainly tells Beneatha that Africa may reflect her heritage, but not his, and 'is nothing but a bunch of raggedy-assed spirituals and some grass huts.'

## BLENDING TWO CULTURES THROUGH MARRIAGE

On another level, George is not sensitive enough to notice that Beneatha's intellectual as well as physical needs have to be stroked. Asagai, on the other hand, appeals to Beneatha's intellectual and psychological needs. Beneatha is at the stage where she wants to feel at ease and be encouraged to philosophize and express her opinions.

In Act III of *A Raisin in the Sun*, Asagai tries to comfort Beneatha when she reveals her unhappiness because her brother, Walter, has misused the money set aside for her college education. She predicts that things will be just the same in Africa when the black man is in power. Asagai replies that at least it will be the black man's fate, determined by himself and the substance of truth, rather than by only Western standards of civilization. . . . This philosophy and Asagai's proposal leave Beneatha confused and shaken, which is an attestation of Lorraine Hansberry's own confused notions of the role of intercultural marriages. . . .

Lorraine Hansberry . . . maintains a romanticized vision of the possibility of such marriages. One assumes that Asagai wants to marry Beneatha . . . in order to complete the passage from his traditional culture to the new world of modernism and change, for he leaves Beneatha with the statement: 'As-so this is what the new world hath finally wrought. . .'. As for Beneatha, her concept of Africa is based upon illusions and preconceived notions of what she thinks Africa will be like. At times her ideas about Africa are blown out of proportion, and Asagai does not help to bring her back to reality.

In his autobiographical book, *The Rise and Fall of a Proper Negro*, Leslie Lacy observes the Afro-Americans who flocked to Ghana in the early 1960s in search of their dream world and identities. They:

> . . . soon discovered that our Africa was an illusion, and tried to relate to and love what they saw. The psychologically weak could not make this adjustment; even if he discovers the 'real Africa,' he is unable to embrace it, since it is not the Africa he wants. He would be criticizing himself. And given his understandable insecurities, he is unable and unwilling to do this . . . In short, he cannot dig Africa for what she is—changing, developing, confused, corrupt, beautiful, uncertain, flirting with revolution.

Although Lacy's statement is not in direct reference to the Afro-American/West-African marriage question, it aptly sums up the future of such marriages, if the two people involved cannot accept the real Africa, be willing to make the best of it and compromise, come to terms with their own inadequacies, and possess a self-confidence in *who* and *what* they are.

# The Contrast Between Lena and Ruth

Sheri Parks

The character of Walter's wife, Ruth, is a foil for
Lena's heroism, says Sheri Parks, who teaches at the
University of Maryland's Department of Radio, Television, and Film. In this selection Parks compares
the emotional strength of Lena with the burdened
weariness of Ruth. Lena helps her family by way of
helping herself. She stays strong in the face of difficulties for the sake of her family through her own
high moral principles and her faith and patient
work. Ruth, on the other hand, is depressed by her
life situation because she has helped her family at
her own expense. She is a committed wife and
mother but because of despair is unable to help the
family as much as heroic Lena does.

Mama Younger is the family's and the play's central character. As if to make her more regal, she is introduced last. Her
presence provides a stark contrast to the unrest of the adult
children. Although Ruth bears the closest resemblance to
Mama, Ruth shows that biological motherhood alone does
not make a viable Black Mother. While much older than
Ruth, Mama has none of Ruth's weariness of spirit. Loosely
based upon Hansberry's own mother, she is "full bodied and
strong. She is one of those women of a certain grace and
beauty who wear it so unobtrusively that it takes a while to
notice. . . . Being a woman who has adjusted to many things
in life and overcome many more, her face is full of strength."
In a more general sense she is based upon the archetypal
Black Mother, whom Hansberry, quoting Langston Hughes's
poem "Washerwoman," described as "the black matriarch
incarnate . . . who scrubs floors of a nation in order to create
black diplomats and university professors."

Excerpted from Sheri Parks, "In My Mother's House: Black Feminist Aesthetics, Television, and *A Raisin in the Sun*," in *Theater and Feminist Aesthetics*, edited by Karen
Laughlin and Catherine Schuler (Madison, NJ: Fairleigh Dickinson University Press,
1995). Reprinted by permission of Associated University Presses.

Her children help to define Mama and she considers distance from one's family to be the luxury of others. Ruth suggests that Mama travel alone, not worrying about her family, like rich white women do. In the television production, Mama laughs at this suggestion before she says, "Something always told me I wasn't no rich white woman." Mama's dreams as well as her actions are all oriented to a better life for her children. She does not buy a new house in a white suburb for artificially politicized reasons, but to get the best house for her family for the money she has. Houses in areas for blacks are further out and much more expensive. Mama is also interested in her own survival and in growth for her sake and for her family's sake. In the face of widespread poverty and disenfranchisement, survival of the body and spirit are central individual concerns for black women. Although the emotional support of one's family is central to the individual's emotional survival, the black woman's role in the physical survival of her family dictates that she find multiple ways to stay physically and emotionally functional in the face of adversity. She must find her personal strength if she and her family are to survive. A lack of strength can be devastating to the woman and, eventually, to the family.

## SETTLED RUTH

Ruth, the "good" and long-suffering wife who is not as strong or as spiritually supported as Mama, most closely approximates the role of the completely family oriented wife-mother who tries to get through life without a sense of self. About thirty, she "was a pretty girl, even exceptionally so.... Now disappointment has already begun to hang in her face." Hansberry notes that in a few years she will be a "settled woman," which on its surface, simply means a married, middle-aged woman. But here marriage and middle age also carry a weariness and disappointment that comes with settling for less than one had hoped. Ruth is so tired of this life that she wakes up sleepy. Hansberry's notes direct the actress to play the role of Ruth with a strong undertone of weariness. She speaks "like someone disinterested and old." While Hansberry describes Ruth's weariness, she also immediately shows her dogged determination and pained energy with her son and her anger at her husband as she tries to jumpstart them for the day.

Ruth constantly thinks in terms of family. What is Ruth's personal dream? Where does *her* rage go? We never know.

She seems to live for her family and, unlike Mama, *through* her family. (Mama does not fear Walter's disapproval or change her actions to the point that all her plans are lost.) Although Ruth has a job, she is the only character who seems to almost never leave home, the exception being her preliminary visit to the abortionist. Her only creations are two children, and she almost loses both. Travis is quickly gaining a life of his own and is testing the limits of his autonomy, and she comes close to aborting the baby, despite her own wishes. Involvement without power or personal strength is an emotionally draining experience. Although Ruth is capable of gentleness and motherly humor with Travis and with Walter, her moods also change rapidly, from humor to brusqueness, perhaps because she is struggling to maintain the appearance of emotional equilibrium without the supports that are useful to her mother-in-law. She speaks of her life as a burdensome one, "I got too much on me this morning."

When Mama remembers her life in the South with its gardens and different life, she asks Ruth to sing "No Ways Tired." Ruth collapses. The title and lyrics of the spiritual which Ruth never gets to sing and are not included in the script would not be lost on a black audience:

> I don't feel no ways tired.
> I've come too far from where I started from.
> No body tole me that the road would be easy.
> I don't believe he brought me this far to leave me.

The lyrics speak of surviving an arduous journey by the ability to draw strength from religious belief. Mama has the ability and is the stronger for it. Ruth does not and suffers for it.

# CHAPTER 4

# Universal Themes in the Play

# Fatalism and Idealism

David D. Cooper

David D. Cooper is an English professor at Michigan
State University. Here he discusses how Beneatha
and Asagai use geometry to understand the human
condition. Her vision of the future as a closed circle
and his vision of the future as an infinite line are
metaphors for the universal experience of pessimism
and optimism, despair and hope, fatalism and idealism. *A Raisin in the Sun,* says Cooper, demonstrates
ways in which people can see the best in situations
as well as the worst, the infinite line as well as the
closed circle.

> When duty whispers low, "Thou Must"
> The youth replies, "I Can!"
>
> *—Ralph Waldo Emerson*

Few modern American plays better capture the essence of
Emerson's claim for moral exuberance that galvanizes
youthful idealism than Lorraine Hansberry's *A Raisin in the
Sun.* Set against a backdrop of overt racism and pervasive
housing discrimination in the 1950s, Hansberry's play manages to recover and sustain ethical idealism amid conditions, personal and societal, that would make fatalistic surrender understandable. It does so without sentimentality
and in spite of the unresolved conflicts and uncertainties
that are left over at the play's end, which remain Hansberry's
legacy to the continuing struggle for racial justice and decency in America. It is a play about distress, futility, and
tragedy, but also about hope and pride and what kind of con-
viction and commitment it takes to bring hope out of hope-
lessness, courage out of fear, and idealism out of fatalism.
[In his book *The Moral Life of Children*] Robert Coles speaks
of the black family—the Youngers—and their ordeal of trying to move out of a segregated Chicago borough as a "con-
tinual tension between hope and despair in people who have

Excerpted from David D. Cooper, "Hansberry's *A Raisin in the Sun," The Explicator,*
vol. 52, no. 1 (Fall 1993), pp. 59–61. Reprinted with permission from the Helen Dwight
Reid Educational Foundation. Published by Heldref Publications, 1319 18th St. NW,
Washington, DC 20036-1802. Copyright © 1993.

had such a rough time and whose prospects are by no means cheerful." Nowhere in the play is that tension more gripping than in the penultimate scene between Asagai and Beneatha Younger, a scene that Robert Nemiroff, who produced and adapted many of Hansberry's works, describes [in *Raisin*'s Introduction] as capturing "the larger statement of the play—and the ongoing struggle it portends."

## FROM IDEALISM TO CYNICISM

After Beneatha's brother Walter Lee squanders, on an ill-advised investment, the life insurance money set aside for Beneatha's medical education, she gives in to despair, even cynicism, watching her dream of becoming a doctor seemingly go up in smoke. Beneatha had always pinned her personal aspirations and her hopes for a more equitable and compassionate society on the prospect of becoming a doctor, reflecting Hansberry's belief that social idealism—the commitment to a better society—is intimately tied to individual moral obligation: that social justice is the collective expression of idealism deeply felt by individuals. "I always thought," Beneatha says to Asagai, that being a doctor "was the one concrete thing in the world that a human being could do. Fix up the sick, you know—and make them whole again."

Once the fragile bond of commitment between her aspirations and society's common welfare is broken, however, Beneatha quickly retrenches into cynicism. "I wanted to cure," Beneatha explains to Asagai. "It used to be so important to me. . . . I used to care. I mean about people and how their bodies hurt. . . ." When Asagai asks her to explain why she stopped caring, Beneatha comes of age, so to speak, morally. "Because [doctoring] doesn't seem deep enough, close enough to what ails mankind! It was a child's way of seeing things—or an idealist's."

At just this point, the play pivots delicately on the moral fulcrum that Coles positions between hope and despair or, put in a socioethical idiom, between idealism and fatalism. Asagai, a patriot for an independent Africa, steps forward to defend hope and idealism. "Children," he reminds Beneatha, "see things very well sometimes—and idealists even better." Beneatha counters, bitterly fatalistic: "You with all your talk and dreams about [a free] Africa! You still think you can patch up the world. Cure the Great Sore of Colonialism—

with the Penicillin of Independence—!... What about all the crooks and thieves and just plain idiots who will come into power and steal and plunder the same as before—only now they will be black ... —WHAT ABOUT THEM?!"

Hansberry quickly synthesizes the moral dilemma into two very precise images:

> BENEATHA: Don't you see there isn't any real progress, Asagai, there is only one large circle that we march in, around and around, each of us with our own little picture in front of us— our own little mirage that we think is the future.
>
> ASAGAI: It isn't a circle—it is simply a long line—as in geometry, you know, one that reaches into infinity. And because we cannot see the end—we also cannot see how it changes. And it is very odd but those who see the changes—who dream, who will not give up—are called idealists . . . and those who see only the circle—we call *them* the "realists."

How one imagines the shape of the future—whether as another version of the present or as a limitless plain of possibilities for personal and societal change—dictates one's solution to the central problem of moral life and whether one draws upon the resources of idealism or "realism"—as Asagai defines it here—insofar as moral action and ethical commitment are concerned. Hansberry makes her choice. Beneatha decides to become a doctor in Africa. The Younger family reaches down for the courage to integrate a white neighborhood. Without addressing the important complexities and ambivalence of those decisions, they represent the courage and moral resourcefulness that were both instrumental in, and essential to, the successes of the following decade's Civil Rights struggles. Among white liberals, for example, the Youngers' decision to move becomes the essence of what liberalism stood for during that time, namely, that racial integration was simultaneously the empowerment of black Americans and the salvation of white America. In his commentary on *A Raisin in the Sun*, Robert Nemiroff lifts the play to this higher level of sociomoral analysis.

> For at the deepest level it is not a specific situation but the human condition, human aspiration and human relationship— the persistence of dreams, of the bonds and conflicts between men and women, parents and children, old ways and new, and the endless struggle against human oppression, whatever the forms it may take, and for individual fulfillment, recognition, and liberation—that are at the heart of such plays. It is not surprising therefore that in each generation we recognize ourselves in them anew.

# A Family Drama

Tom Scanlan

Teacher and critic Tom Scanlan is the author of *Family, Drama, and American Dreams,* from which this selection comes. He groups Lorraine Hansberry's *A Raisin in the Sun* with works of other famous American playwrights like Eugene O'Neill, Arthur Miller, and Tennessee Williams, who are all concerned with family life and the relationships within families. Their plays focus on attempts to achieve individual fulfillment as well as family harmony. *Raisin* emphasizes the need for balance when it comes to personal independence versus group involvement. Unlike most other plays in this American tradition of family drama, however, Hansberry uses humor and other devices to create "a potential for turning agitation to interaction." The family in *Raisin* is not so much a hindrance to its members as it is in O'Neill, Miller, and Williams, but a vehicle for personal change and growth. However, writes Scanlan, at times Hansberry's tactics come "perilously close to being turned into a theatrical joke."

The best of [the] plays of black family life is still Lorraine Hansberry's *A Raisin in the Sun* (1959). . . . Hansberry writes a realistic social drama of the struggle for life by little people, in this case the Youngers, a black family which is crowded into an apartment. . . . They have, as one member of the family puts it, "acute ghetto-itus." Here, too, the family is held together by a strong mother, Lena, known as Mama; and the dead father-figure provides the possibility for change in their lives through the legacy of his insurance money. But escape from family is not the solution or even, really, the issue. Instead, the play celebrates the family as the anchor by which the individual maintains pride, sense of purpose, and resilience in the face of social injustice and personal despair.

Excerpted from *Family, Drama, and American Dreams,* by Tom Scanlan. Copyright © 1978 by Tom Scanlan. Reproduced with permission from Greenwood Publishing Group, Inc., Westport, Conn.

For Mama, the four generations of Youngers and the example of her dead husband, Big Walter, have made her own struggles worthwhile; in fact, her family heritage has made survival possible by giving her an example of dignity and integrity. Her son, Walter, discovers the same resource. In the end he must decide if he will take money, which he desperately wants, from whites who wish to keep the Youngers out of the neighborhood. Mama forces him to make that decision in front of his own son:

> WALTER: What I am telling you is that we called you over here to tell you that we are very proud and that this is—this is my son, who makes the sixth generation of our family in this country, and that we have all thought about your offer and we have decided to move into our house because my father—my father—he earned it. (*MAMA has her eyes closed and is rocking back and forth as though she were in church, with her head nodding the amen yes.*)

To Walter, the concrete fact of being together with his son has significance in itself and beyond itself. This double meaning gives him the strength to throw off his cynicism and to achieve his manhood. The moment is personal, familial, and timeful.

If Hansberry sees the family as a resource, her celebration of it tries not to ignore or gloss over the real tensions among the Youngers. From Mama's first entrance on stage, we can see the potential for tyranny in her strong character. Mama's dominance is a balance of forces. Her severity with her daughter Beneatha's flippant remarks on religion is as much an indication of the daughter's immaturity as it is the mother's overbearing nature. Lena has earned the right to her beliefs by trying to live them; her daughter has no genuine reason to challenge them, only a sophomore's sophistication. Similarly, Walter's plan to make something of himself involves obtaining a liquor store license by graft and hustling, activities his mother distrusts. Not only are they morally suspect to her but they are outside the family experience and competence. The very extravagance of Walter's dreams and fantasies of business life shows how naive and innocent he is as a wheeler-dealer, a perfect mark. Walter and Beneatha talk about being grown-up, but if Mama dominates them it is in part because their actions do not bear out their words. They demand freedom, but Hansberry measures the legitimacy of that demand as well as Mama's too great strength.

## FAMILY DYNAMICS

*A Raisin in the Sun* has, then, a conflict between security and freedom. Hansberry is working toward a new formulation of this dilemma. She is beginning to explore its creative possibilities along with its destructive side. Dramatically, this potential is embodied in the rather simple ability of the characters to learn from each other, to change in reaction to claims made on them which they initially resist. When Mama and Walter are deadlocked—she with her need to keep the family secure and he with his need for personal achievement—we are faced with a situation of family counterclaims typical in American drama. At this point the tradition suggests several possible resolutions. Walter could break loose from Mama and emerge as the hero of the new black consciousness which frees itself from family ties and an older, debilitating habit of mind. If the emphasis was on Mama in this action, we would have the pattern of the Lomans [Arthur Miller's family in *Death of a Salesman*]; if it was on Walter, we would have something closer to the Bergers [Clifford Odets's family in *Awake and Sing!*]. If Walter broke free but wounded his psyche in the process, we would be reminded of the Wingfields [Tennessee Williams's family in *The Glass Menagerie*]. On the other hand, if no break occurs, several other patterns are available. Perhaps the family would be shown as an hypocrisy, as in later [Lillian] Hellman and [Edward] Albee (in works which appeared about the same time); or we could be witnessing a replay of one of O'Neill's families—the heroic isolation of the Cabots [*Desire Under the Elms*], the mutual destruction of the Mannons [*Mourning Becomes Electra*], or the inescapable love and hate of the Tyrones [*Long Day's Journey Into Night*].

## HANSBERRY'S NEW APPROACH

The value of *A Raisin in the Sun* is in Hansberry's attempt to work out a somewhat different pattern, one which recognizes both claims but sees their interaction as a matter of continuing possibility rather than as a fixed dilemma. Mama's character is not rigid but capable of change. She can be more than one sort of person and can act in a different way. She learns and changes, and we see the effect of this first with Beneatha and then with Walter. Walter, too, has this capability, which depends on the family context. The family does not represent a fixed psychological set or a metaphysical certainty but a potential for turning agitation to interaction.

Hansberry effectively achieves this sense of possibility indirectly, through the rich vein of humor which runs through the play. Humor is a strategy of survival for the characters, a way by which they keep themselves in balance and restore their resilience in the face of difficult circumstances. Its effect on the play is to cut through the impossibility of a situation and to release forces in new ways. Hansberry seems to be saying that people do funny things (as well as admirable and stupid things) because of their needs. All these possibilities exist at a given moment.

The humor in *A Raisin in the Sun* is one of its strong elements and gives more credibility to a play which in other ways is not as rich and evocative as it needs to be to fulfill its own promise. The family drama here is worth our attention because of the new direction in which Hansberry tries to take it, not because she manages to travel a long ways in that direction. Her achievement is limited. The emphasis on the potential for change in her characters is handled too simply and so runs the risk of sentimentality. Hansberry senses that the tension between freedom and security in the family might be a humanizing one in that either impulse has the possibility of qualifying the worst effects of the other. But she does not dramatize this possibility so much as dramatize her faith in its existence. The question is how agitation becomes interaction. The answer, dramatically, comes in the imposition of the character of Mama. Her superiority is the mechanism by which Hansberry makes certain that the right change takes place. Because of Mama's relative strength, the actual risks to the family are reduced and what could be hard-won knowledge begins to look like a vindication of faith. At the end Walter and Beneatha leave the stage quarreling as they did at the beginning, *"and the anger is hard and real till their voices diminish,"* says Hansberry in the stage directions. But Mama and Ruth, her daughter-in-law, are on stage chuckling and smiling at them, which serves to insulate us from their anger. Hansberry's insight that the conflicts and struggles will go on, that the issue could be not harmony but the capacity to make something of tension, comes perilously close to being turned into a theatrical joke—oops, here we go again.

A similar weakness exists in Mama's assertion of love for Walter when he is about to sell out the family heritage. This ought to be a difficult moment for Mama, too, since Walter is threatening to destroy the most cherished value in her world. But Hansberry does not show a struggle within Mama. Rather, the depth of Mama's love (in an earlier scene, the depth of her religious faith) is contrasted with the superficiality of Beneatha's reaction. Nothing can shake Mama's love. But what, then, of the possibility for change? Love becomes *the* solution rather than a resource, the danger that Walter will "dry up/Like a raisin in the sun" is reduced and we watch his final test comforted rather than fearful. In another context, there might be a vitalizing danger in the last sentences of Mama's speech on love: "When you starts measuring somebody, measure him right, child, measure him right. Make sure you done taken account what hills and valleys he come through before he got to wherever he is."

Hansberry is edging toward an interesting paradox: if measurement of Walter by Mama is a real possibility, then measurement is also more powerful and believable as a source of strength for Walter. But unless Walter also can fail by the standard of Mama's family ethic, the drama soothes us instead of exploring the way in which two warring elements—in this case, judgment and love—can be sustaining and their tension turned to energy and strength.

# Similar Themes in Hansberry and O'Casey

Peter L. Hays

Peter L. Hays, author of books on Ernest Hemingway and on the grotesque in literature, writes about the similarities between Irish playwright Sean O'Casey's play *Juno and the Paycock* and American playwright Lorraine Hansberry's *A Raisin in the Sun*. Both involve the family, social injustice, poverty, and aspirations gone awry. Both focus on universal themes of the human condition—and "human dignity, heroic assertion, and a wail of pain [are] much alike in Dublin or Chicago's Southside," writes Hays. *Raisin* shares *Juno*'s realism about social conditions. However, its ending differs significantly from that of the Irish play in that O'Casey finds nothing to celebrate but endurance, while Hansberry finally offers affirmation and hope beyond mere endurance.

Lorraine Hansberry states in *To Be Young, Gifted and Black* (Englewood, 1969) that her introduction to the power of drama—as opposed to its imaginative appeal on the printed page—occurred at the University of Wisconsin. She was intensely moved at a performance because, though the play's setting was across the Atlantic, the time before her birth, and the race of the characters different from her own, she recognized their pain, their heartache, their suffering:

> I remember sitting there stunned with a melody that I thought might have been sung in a different meter. The play was *Juno*, the writer Sean O'Casey—but the melody was one that I had known for a very long while.
>
> I was seventeen and I did not think then of *writing* the melody as *I* knew it—in a different key; but I believed it entered my consciousness and stayed there ... (Miss Hansberry's ellipsis)

This reminiscence is followed in the book by a passage from Miss Hansberry's first play, *Raisin in the Sun*, where she did

Reprinted from Peter L. Hays, "*A Raisin in the Sun* and *Juno and the Paycock*," *Phylon*, vol. 33, no. 2 (Summer 1972), pp. 175–76, by permission of *Phylon*.

indeed write the melody as she knew it, incorporating, un-doubtedly, autobiography, but incorporating also elements from this play of O'Casey's that had moved her so much.

The first noticeable parallel is the one provided in the text: it shows us first Joxer drunk and carried away by song, while long-suffering Juno looks on; then Walter Younger drunkenly, atavistically asserting his manhood, while Ruth goes on with her ironing. Commented Miss Hansberry,

> . . . When you believe people so completely—because *every-body* has their drunkards and their braggarts and their cow-ards, you know—then you also believe in their moments of heroic assertion: you don't doubt them.

### BOYLE/HANSBERRY: POINT/COUNTERPOINT

*A letter to the editor from an Irishman accused Hansberry of plagiarizing* Raisin *from O'Casey, prompting Hans-berry to respond in a way that bears on the universality of the play.*

*To the Drama Editor:*

I finally saw "Raisin in the Sun," and it is so clear to me—now—that, although it finally departs from the great man's spirit, the Lorraine Hansberry play "owes" so much to Sean O'Casey's "Juno and the Paycock" that it should at least say it was "suggested" by the latter.

The will "bit," the treacherous friend (right out of Joxer), the Poitier drunk scene, the arch "sister," and even the sharp line: "Eat your eggs" (O'Casey has it "Eat your sassidge, man") are straight from O'Casey.

I remember when "The Skin of Our Teeth" appeared. Wilder was clobbered by James Joyce fans for "owing" much less to Joyce than Miss Hansberry's apparently does to O'Casey—a reading of both plays will reveal even more similarities (the Junoesque mother, and her God-fearing, for instance).

I wonder whether other playgoers see the similarities I have mentioned. If so, the O'Casey Club should see the Green Crow is treated right.

A. Boyle, Los Angeles, Calif.

### AUTHOR'S REPLY

*To the Drama Editor:*

One of the prime features of a segregated society is the in-evitable development of ignorance of the respective ways of the two isolated halves of that society. . . .

And this belief, of course, is what she wanted to communicate in *Raisin.* As she wrote to her mother, two nights before the play opened:

> Mama, it is a play that tells the truth about people, Negroes and life and I think it will help a lot of people to understand how we are just as complicated as they are—and just as mixed up—but above all, that we have among our miserable and downtrodden ranks—people who are the very essence of human dignity. That is what, after all the laughter and tears, the play is supposed to say.

And, of course, it does—like O'Casey's plays, and Shakespeare's and those of many lesser playwrights. But *Raisin*

---

The fact of the peculiar structure of the Negro family, historically developed from slavery, presumably, is not as well known as we might otherwise suppose. The matriarchy in Negro life is such an entrenched characteristic, at once beloved and hated, that it would not occur to a Negro student of drama to search for the origins of a "Junoesque" mother in a play of Negro life. It is more difficult to imagine "Raisin" without Lena Younger than with her; she is not fabricated from another dramatist, she is overtly imposed from life. One may meet her at least a dozen times on a casual stroll through the Negro community, anywhere in the United States any afternoon. Moreover, her "God fearing" components are as necessary to the truth of her character as those grim, beige-colored cotton stockings she is utterly dedicated to.

My reactions to Mr. Boyle's other remarks cannot help but be more frivolous and, I suppose, impudent. This is borne of the notion that surely drunkenness, the eating of eggs and sausages, and the having of sisters must be known wherever men know thirst and frustration, hunger and familial relationships. For all of my admiration of Irish culture, I cannot believe that it must alone lay claim to allusions to those matters in dialogue or dramaturgy. I join Mr. O'Casey, above all, in a hearty chuckle at the thought that anyone would think so.

As a matter of fact, I am the first to say that my play and all plays I shall ever write "owe" deeply to the great O'Casey. Precisely, however, where Mr. Boyle suggests departure: in the spirit.

Lorraine Hansberry, New York

"Mailbag/O'Casey/Hansberry," *New York Times,* 2.1:x5 (28 June 1959).

has more in common with *Juno* than just human dignity, heroic assertion, and a wail of pain much alike in Dublin or Chicago's Southside.

## THE YOUNGERS AND THE BOYLES

First, both plays are set in urban tenements, and both involve families as protagonists—not just the parents or children, with the other generation as necessary for realism and dramatic complication—but the family as a whole. Its actions when a member is lost—when Johnny is killed, the Captain defects with Joxer, or when Walter Lee decides to capitulate to Mr. Charlie—creates the tensions and dimensions of plays and the characters.

In both works, strong women support their families psychologically and monetarily—in *Raisin,* because Walter Lee, Sr., is dead; in *Juno,* because Jack Boyle is allergic to work. Each family has a bright daughter with intellectual pretensions and a passion for women's rights, who is courted by a dull suitor for marriage whom she does not love and by one she finds more attractive. Both families are plagued with fair-weather friends, and both plays end with a younger woman pregnant with a child that will be a financial burden. Each play is lightened by song and dance, and each makes pointed reference to its social context: the one set in the midst of the Irish rebellion against English rule, the other set at the beginnings of the current black rebellion for self-rule.

## THE FAMILIES' LEGACIES

Perhaps the most visible similarity is the device of the legacy: both families wait with hope for the money that will solve their problems and give them the opportunity to escape the ghetto of possibilities in which they live. In both cases the legacy falls through—in *Juno* it never arrives, due to the lawyer's stupidity, although the Boyles have already spent much of it on credit; in *Raisin* Walter is fleeced out of most of the insurance money when he insists on investing in a scheme his mother warned him against. The difference is the outcome and the melody. Without the money, Jack Boyle, the Captain, escapes deeper into alcoholic stupor. His son is killed and Boyle does not even know. Only Juno retains her pride and her strength as she takes Mary away to care for her. O'Casey's dominant purpose is social criticism—pointing out the internal flaws and internecine wrangling that the Irish would have to overcome in order to prosper. In *Raisin* on the other hand, the loss of outside help, of a *deus ex machina,* results in Walter Lee's finding himself and restoring a patriarchy to the Younger family.

The difference may lie in the resilience of Walter's youth, in that he has fewer illusions to deceive himself with than the Captain does, or in Lena Younger's wisdom in leading as well as pushing. Nevertheless, Miss Hansberry is no less realistic than O'Casey. Only the deposit has been made on the house and each of the Youngers will have to work to make the payments, and their all white neighborhood will not be Nirvana. But *Raisin* ends on hope, not just endurance. The melody is not that of a keen [lamentation], its tempo is too upbeat.

# The Psychology of Adjusting to Reality

George R. Adams

George R. Adams was an English professor at Wisconsin State University–Whitewater when this article was published in 1971. He discusses the need for Americans of all races to create an identity for themselves that adheres to their notions—and their society's notions—of an accepted value system. In the case of the Younger family, it is an all-American set of values, which stresses the individual's opportunity to achieve economic success through hard work and respectable behavior. But because of social inequities, writes Adams, "one adopts [ways] to legally and ethically cope with them while fitting into the basically benevolent democratic society." This process of socialization is ultimately a psychological one, a maturing that involves recognizing harsh realities while continuing to strive to be a good citizen.

*A Raisin in the Sun* is an ego-play in that it describes how a Black family comes to the right relationship with "reality." The family, the Youngers, consists of Lena, the widowed mother, her son, Walter Lee, his wife, Ruth, his son, Travis, and his sister, Beneatha, all living in a Chicago ghetto tenement sometime in the early 1950's. Big Walter, the father, has recently died and, as the play opens, the Younger family is waiting for the $10,000 insurance check. Lena has plans for the money: to put a down-payment on a house in an all-white suburb, Clybourne Park. Moreover, she has plans for the others. Beneatha is to marry a rich Negro, George Murchison; Walter is to be a strong and proud worker, like his father, and not the liquor salesman he wants to be; Ruth is to quit working; Travis is to have fresh air and a yard to play in; and Lena is to have a garden. Unfortunately, events

Excerpted from George R. Adams, "Black Militant Drama," *American Imago*, vol. 28, no. 2 (Summer 1971), pp. 109–15. Copyright © 1971 The Johns Hopkins University Press. Reprinted with permission.

interfere. Ruth is pregnant again and is considering an abortion, Beneatha is interested in a young Nigerian nationalist, Joseph Asagai, and Walter is obsessed with making money. To save her family, Lena gives most of the insurance money to Walter; but he loses it to a confidence man.

In despair, Walter plans to sell back the Clybourne Park house at a profit to a representative of a white citizens' council. At this critical point, only Lena's strength saves them. When Walter cries, "There ain't nothing but taking in this world, and he who takes most is smartest" and prepares to literally get down on his knees to the white man, Lena replies, "Nobody in my family never let nobody pay 'em no money that was a way of telling us we wasn't fit to walk the earth. . . . We ain't never been that dead inside." But she tells Beneatha, who is contemptuous of Walter, "Have you cried for that boy today? . . . When you starts measuring somebody, measure him right, child. . . . Make sure you done taken into account what hills and valleys he come through before he got to wherever he is." Walter, shamed but strengthened, tells the Clybourne Park representative, "This is my son, who makes the sixth generation of our family in this country . . . and we have decided to move into our house." And they do, facing an uncertain, but not dark, future.

## NOT A BLACK PLAY

It can be asked, If *A Raisin in the Sun* is oriented to reality, why does Walter willingly give up those things, i.e., independence and economic success, which we are told are real social and moral values in America? And how can the Youngers' moving into a white suburb be called "reality" and not wish-fulfillment? As a partial answer to these questions, let us look for a moment at some characteristics of the play. First, it is apparent that *A Raisin in the Sun* is not necessarily a Black play; that is, none of the personality traits of the Youngers, none of their goals, and none of their troubles and successes are specifically those of Black people in Chicago of the 1950's. As Norman Podhoretz once remarked about Arthur Miller's *Death of a Salesman,* Lorraine Hansberry's play could be a Jewish play rewritten for a white gentile audience. . . . It is perhaps not inevitable that in the 1950's, a working-class Jewish family would be discouraged from moving to the Eden of the *goyim,* the suburbs, but it is possible; moreover, the play has few chronological allusions, so that if we read it as a play of the 1940's, then anti-Semitism would function thematically. At any rate, the family structure of the play could certainly be Jewish; Walter's speech about generations, Beneatha's desire to be a doctor, the young idealist, Asagai (a "Zionist"), all could come out of a drama dealing with the break-up of the tight, "Jewish-mama" dominated American-Jewish family under the social pressures of modern gentile America. . . . In summary, then, the condition of the Youngers is for us "universal," that is, it represents what we conceive to be common lot of a good many "ethnic" groups and celebrates the basic unit of American social structure, the nuclear family with a dominant and wise parent-figure.

## A "NATURALISTIC" WORK

The second "universal" characteristic of the play is sociological. For the Youngers, the correct "adjustment to life" consists of their facing the "facts of life" on three levels. The first level is sociological, that of the Black man's condition in 1950's America as defined for us by studies such as *Black Rage*. Sociologically "true" also is the ghetto milieu of the Youngers, the large family crowded into a too-small, run-down tenement apartment. The second level is literary. Black "matriarch," Lena, the product of sociological studies of the fatherless ghetto family, is reinforced by the literary type of the "enduring" Black mother popularized by Southern white writers; reinforcing this image is the culturally-acceptable figure of the educative mother. The third realistic level is economic, the struggle of the lower class for survival, a struggle made more difficult by color, lack of education and training, and familial pressures. In short, *A Raisin in the Sun*, as literature, makes use of all the documentary resources which went into the literary tradition of American "Naturalism."

A naturalistic work presents what the society would only reluctantly accept as reality if it were not forced to do so by the data of social science and the skill and passion of the artist. In practice, such works fuse "unpleasant" but documented sociological data with a familiar literary form (here, a three-act structure, careful detail, contemporary speech), so that we are made to feel the "reality" of the presented society. But it is not our response to the sociologically and esthetically "true" levels of reality in the play which is the important conscious response; we respond also to an ideological level of reality in the play, the bourgeois reality-definitions which Lorraine Hansberry either introjected and unconsciously incorporated into her play or deliberately exploited.

## EGO-DEVELOPMENT IN THE FREE WORLD

As I pointed out earlier, it would seem that Walter's giving up his dream of economic success is a rejection of the white bourgeois value system. But for most white Americans, the equation of easy if somewhat immoral money with the basic American ethic is a "radical" equation. Even those Americans who are conscious of disparities between the theory and practice of American capitalist-competitive democratic society tend to look upon the disparities as accidental, superficial, and open to correction, in short, as not inherent in the systems. . . .

The model (or topography of social reality) is roughly this: in America everyone, including ghetto Blacks, is legally and morally free to develop his own life-pattern; of course, given the nature of human existence, psychological and social, there are difficulties and obligations involved in this self-development. The difficulties stem from the resistance of people (racists) who are oriented to the superficial characteristics of humans, or the disparities in employment generated by the functioning of free enterprise, or the delays in civil rights, caused by the necessarily slow and precise working of justice, or the misunderstandings (e.g., about equality) caused by temporary ignorance. The obligations are imposed by "maturity," that is, the correct analysis of social difficulties, and the patient means one adopts to legally and ethically cope with them while fitting into the basically benevolent democratic society. Thus "facing reality" is a twofold process, involving a perception of disparities and a commitment to the underlying American ethic of freedom and justice, brotherhood and labor, respect and obedience. In short, "facing reality," "growing up," and "becoming a responsible citizen" are synonymous, and this activity in turn is synonymous with correct ego-development.

As Freud points out, we "mature," in the European bourgeois definition of the term, by building an ego-structure strong enough to cope with and define reality. Ego-construction in its early stages depends in large part on reality-representatives, in effect miniature versions of the whole society, namely, the authoritative and educative family leaders, the mother and father. By imitation and forced obedience, the child learns certain "facts" about living in the "real" world: the force of authority, the necessity for punishment, the approval of obedient behavior, the rewards of work meaningful to the dominant authority, the existence of aggression. Along with these introjected values, which are common to most Americans of whatever ethnic or class background, are specific primary cultural values transmitted by family and society; in white culture they include pride, piety, loyalty, education, monogamy. This is the "legitimate" model of reality to which the Younger family adheres, and so we, like Walter, respond to the play as a true paradigm of reality-adjustment. Under the guidance of the parent, Lena, Walter is strengthened by his recognition of certain facts of life, namely that Black Americans have a social right (to move out of the ghetto into the white suburbs), a psychological necessity (to direct frustration outward into healthy aggression, manifested as self-assertion and hard work), a social duty (to reinforce the values of mature citizen responsibility and the American democratic ethic), an economic responsibility (to invest money wisely), and a personal and familial obligation (pride in oneself and one's forebears). With Lena's help, Walter learns what it means to become a responsible father and a good citizen. . . .

## A WHITE VALUE SYSTEM

It is clear that what occurs on the conscious, social level (Walter's becoming mature, responsible, and normal) is the same activity which occurs in introjecting the correct societal-familial value-system, a value-system passed down from Big Walter through Lena. In the world created by *A Raisin in the Sun,* the value-system is White. It is therefore surprising, momentarily, to turn to the epigraph of the play, drawn from a poem by the Black poet Langston Hughes: "What happens to a dream deferred? / Does it dry up / like a raisin in the sun?/ Or fester like a sore— / And then run? . . . *Or does it explode?"* The title of the play would suggest that a dream deferred dries up; but the Youngers' family dream, as distinct from that of Walter, is not deferred, or at least only temporarily. Walter will not get rich, but he is once again head of the family, and they are out of the ghetto. Ruth must go back to work, but she now has a goal; Beneatha may not become a doctor, but she may help to build a nation. Thus, the title is puzzling. But one thing is certain: the Youngers are not going to explode in a rebellious, id-response to oppressive white power. They see the white value-system as real and no longer permanently oppressive; so does the approving audience of the play. In the play, the mature ego must adjust to "genuine" white values; Black revolutionaries or rebels are "immature," id-controlled children, with a distorted definition (or rejection) of reality and responsible behavior.

# To Be Black, Female, and Universal

Margaret B. Wilkerson

Though Hansberry wrote as a black woman, she wrote for neither blacks nor women in particular, but for humanity in general. In this selection, Margaret B. Wilkerson emphasizes Hansberry's central role in addressing issues affecting both genders, many racial groups, and people in various socio-economic positions. Attaching equal importance to the plight of all people, Hansberry observes that being denigrated as the "other" is a universal experience. Thus the "conflict" between specific and universal meaning is false. Hansberry was deeply committed to the belief that it is attention to real specifics like blackness and femaleness that leads to valid universality, and *A Raisin in the Sun* demonstrates it. Margaret B. Wilkerson has taught in the Afro-American Studies Department and served as director of the Center for the Continuing Education of Women at the University of California, Berkeley. A playwright herself, she has also served as director of the Black Theatre Program of the American Theatre Association.

Lorraine Hansberry never accepted the place customarily accorded a black female college drop-out. She achieved unparalleled success by writing *A Raisin in the Sun*, which became the first play by a black woman to be produced on Broadway and to win the New York Drama Critics' Circle Award. Then, even as the critics hailed her new black voice, she shocked them by writing another play—about whites—called *The Sign in Sidney Brustein's Window*, which exposes the spiritual poverty of the Beat generation and calls the disenchanted to social commitment. Even the child Lorraine

Excerpted from Margaret B. Wilkerson, "Lorraine Hansberry: The Complete Feminist," *Freedomways*, vol. 19, no. 4 (1979), pp. 235–38. Reprinted by permission of the author. Footnotes revised by the author.

was unconventional—maintaining an empathy and respect for her less wealthy schoolmates, defying the class separation which is touted as the norm among those who have and those who have not.

Were she writing today, she would be called a feminist. The term, however, would merely obscure her special vision. Today the cross-current of issues between women and men, black and white, forces us into even smaller factions, and the humanistic views of a Lorraine Hansberry could easily be lost in the rush to take sides and profit from the ensuing conflict. The controversies generated by recent books and plays about black women are symbols of our confusion about our own history and present state. Thus, it is very timely to examine the writings of a modern black woman who wrote assertively about women before it was popular to do so. Her conceptions of womanhood and manhood may help to sort out our real from our imaginary problems.

With the statement, "I was born black and a female," Hansberry immediately establishes the basis for a tension that informs her world-view. Her consciousness, of both ethnicity and gender from the very beginning, brought awareness of two key forces of conflict and oppression in the contemporary world. Because she embraces these dual truths despite their implicit competition for her attention (a competition that is exacerbated by external pressures), her vision is expansive enough to contain and even synthesize what to others would be contradictions. Thus, she is amused in 1955 at progressive friends who protest whenever she poses "so much as an itsy-bitsy analogy between the situation, say, of the Negro people in the U.S.—and women." She is astonished to be accused by a woman of being bitter and of thinking that men are beasts simply because she expresses the view that women are oppressed. "Must I hate 'men' any more than I hate 'white people'—because some of them are savage and others commit savage acts," she asks herself. "Of course not!" she answers vehemently.

This recognition of the tension implicit in her blackness and femaleness was the starting point for her philosophical journey from the South Side of Chicago to the world community. The following quote charts that journey and the expansion of Hansberry's consciousness, which is unconstrained by culture and gender, but which at the same time refuses to diminish the importance of either.

I was born on the South Side of Chicago. I was born black and a female. I was born in a depression after one world war, and came into my adolescence during another. While I was still in my teens the first atom bombs were dropped on human beings at Nagasaki and Hiroshima. And by the time I was twenty-three years old, my government and that of the Soviet Union had entered actively into the worst conflict of nerves in human history—the Cold War.

I have lost friends and relatives through cancer, lynching and war. I have been personally the victim of physical attack which was the offspring of racial and political hysteria. I have worked with the handicapped and seen the ravages of congenital diseases that we have not yet conquered, because we spend our time and ingenuity in far less purposeful wars; I have known persons afflicted with drug addiction and alcoholism and mental illness. I see daily on the streets of New York, street gangs and prostitutes and beggars. I have, like all of you, on a thousand occasions seen indescribable displays of man's very real inhumanity to man, and I have come to maturity, as we all must, knowing that greed and malice and indifference to human misery and bigotry and corruption, brutality, and perhaps above all else, ignorance—the prime ancient and persistent enemy of man—abound in this world.

I say all of this to say that one cannot live with sighted eyes and feeling heart and not know and react to the miseries which afflict this world.

Her "sighted eyes and feeling heart" are what enable her to hear the wail of her own people in Sean O'Casey's *Juno and the Paycock*, a play steeped in Irish history and tradition. And those eloquent moans send her forth to capture that collective cry in a black idiom.

## FROM BLACK AND FEMALE TO "EVERYMAN"

Hansberry's cognizance of being black and female form the basis for her comprehensive world-view. For just as she can accept fully the implications and responsibility of both blackness and femaleness, so can she also contain the many other competing and equally legitimate causes which grow out of humankind's misery. Fundamental to this comprehensive world-view, however, is Hansberry's insistence upon a thorough probing of the individual within the specifics of culture, ethnicity and gender. In the midst of her expansiveness, she refuses to diminish the pain, suffering or truths of any one group in order to benefit another, a factor which makes her plays particularly rich and her characters thoroughly complex. Hence, she can write authentically about a black family in *A Raisin in the Sun* and yet produce, in the same instance, a play which appeals to both Blacks and whites, bridging for a moment the historical and cultural gaps between them.

Her universalism, which redefines that much abused term, grows out of a deep, complex encounter with the specific terms of human experience as it occurs for Blacks, women, whites and many other groups of people. Her universalism is not facile, nor does it gloss over the things that divide people. She engages those issues, works through them, to find whatever may be, a priori, the human commonality that lies beneath. It is as if she believes that one can understand and embrace the human family (with all its familial warfare) only to the extent that one can engage the truths (however partisan they may seem) of a social, cultural individual. "We must turn our eyes outward," she wrote, "but to do so we must also turn them inward toward our people and their complex and still transitory culture." When she turns inward, she sees not only color but gender as well—a prism of humanity.

## A RICHNESS OF SPIRIT

Although she recognizes and accepts the discreteness of being black and female, Hansberry also understands their interrelatedness. Spiritually, she is a descendant of early black feminists such as Ida B. Wells and Sojourner Truth, who wrote and spoke compellingly about the plight of the black race—both women and men. They, too, refused to relegate the woman to a "place," emphasizing instead the importance of her full participation in the life and struggles of the race. At the same time, they argued strongly on issues affecting black men—lynching and work conditions in particular. Speaking for women's rights did not cancel out fighting for black men.

When Hansberry looks inward, she also finds a richness of experience and spirit which must be shared with the world.

> Oh, the things that we have learned in this unkind house that we have to tell the world about! *Despair?* Did someone say despair was question in the world? Well then, listen to the sons of those who have know little else, if you wish to know the resilience of this thing you would so quickly resign to mythhood, this thing called the human spirit. . . . *Life?* Ask those who have tasted of it in pieces rationed out by enemies! *Love?*

Ah, ask the troubadours who come from those who have loved when all reason pointed to the uselessness and fool-hardiness of love! Perhaps we shall be the teachers when it is done. Out of the depths of pain we have thought to be our sole heritage in this world—o, we know about love!

Hansberry concludes that she, as a black female writer, has an obligation to participate in the intellectual affairs of people everywhere. Indeed, she has a major contribution to make.

# CHAPTER 5

# The Play in Various Forms

READINGS ON
A RAISIN IN THE SUN

# Broadway, 1959: An Honest Play

Brooks Atkinson

Brooks Atkinson was the longtime *New York Times* theater critic for whom a Broadway theater is named. This is his 1959 review of the original stage production of *A Raisin in the Sun*, starring Sidney Poitier as Walter Younger.

Atkinson points to *Raisin*'s honesty—in the writing, the story, the set, and the acting. Working with a cast that included Ruby Dee, Diana Sands, Claudia McNeil, and Louis Gossett, director Lloyd Richards "directed a bold and stirring performance."

Emphasizing the play's universality, Atkinson compares *A Raisin in the Sun* to the renowned Russian play *The Cherry Orchard* by Anton Chekhov—both in its mixture of the comic with the serious and in its emphasis on how one's environment shapes his or her character.

In "A Raisin in the Sun," which opened at the Ethel Barrymore last evening, Lorraine Hansberry touches on some serious problems. No doubt, her feelings about them are as strong as any one's.

But she has not tipped her play to prove one thing or another. The play is honest. She has told the inner as well as the outer truth about a Negro family in the southside of Chicago at the present time [1959]. Since the performance is also honest and since Sidney Poitier is a candid actor, "A Raisin in the Sun" has vigor as well as veracity and is likely to destroy the complacency of anyone who sees it.

## A TEST OF CHARACTER

The family consists of a firm-minded widow, her daughter, her restless son and his wife and son. The mother has brought up her family in a tenement that is small, battered but personable. All the mother wants is that her children adhere to the code of honor and self-respect that she inherited from her parents.

The son is dreaming of success in a business deal. And the daughter, who is race-conscious, wants to become a physician and heal the wounds of her people. After a long delay the widow receives $10,000 as the premium on her husband's life insurance. The money projects the family into a series of situations that test their individual characters.

What the situations are does not matter at the moment. For "A Raisin the Sun" is a play about human beings who want, on the one hand, to preserve their family pride and, on the other hand, to break out of the poverty that seems to be their fate. Not having any axe to grind, Miss Hansberry has a wide range of topics to write about—some of them hilarious, some of them painful in the extreme.

You might, in fact, regard "A Raisin in the Sun" as a Negro "The Cherry Orchard." Although the social scale of the characters is different, the knowledge of how character is controlled by environment is much the same, and the alternation of humor and pathos is similar.

If there are occasional crudities in the craftsmanship, they are redeemed by the honesty of the writing. And also by the rousing honesty of the stage work. For Lloyd Richards has selected an admirable cast and directed a bold and stirring performance.

## STELLAR PERFORMANCES

Mr. Poitier is a remarkable actor with enormous power that is always under control. Cast as the restless son, he vividly communicates the tumult of a highstrung young man. He is as eloquent when he has nothing to say as when he has a pungent line to speak. He can convey devious processes of thought as graphically as he can clown and dance.

As the matriarch, Claudia McNeil gives a heroic performance. Although the character is simple, Miss McNeil gives it nobility of spirit. Diana Sands' amusing portrait of the overintellectualized daughter; Ivan Dixon's quiet, sagacious student from Nigeria; Ruby Dee's young wife burdened with problems; Louis Gossett's supercilious suitor; John Fiedler's timid white man, who speaks sanctimonious platitudes— bring variety and excitement to a first-rate performance.

## SIMPLE HONESTY

All the crises and comic sequences take place inside Ralph Alswang's set, which depicts both the poverty and the taste of the family. Like the play, it is honest. That is Miss Hansberry's personal contribution to an explosive situation in which simple honesty is the most difficult thing in the world. And also the most illuminating.

# Comparing the 1961 Film and the Unfilmed Screenplay

Margaret B. Wilkerson

Margaret B. Wilkerson, an expert in African American studies and black theater, discusses the differences among the original play, the screenplay Hansberry wrote for the film version, and the final film (which starred the cast from the stage production). Calling director Dan Petrie's film "a thing of beauty," Hansberry praises the work but makes a distinction between it and her own vision for the film. Petrie's finished product is essentially a filmed version of the stage play, with most of the action set in the Younger household. Hansberry's screenplay, on the other hand, makes use of panoramic cityscapes and montages that take the characters out of their living room and into the world of the Chicago they inhabit. Her goal was to develop her characters by showing them going about their daily lives and interacting with others, including those who patronize them in subtly racist ways. Most of her additional scenery and development of social background ended up being cut from the film, mainly for the sake of time. But Wilkerson believes many of the cuts were political in nature: The movie studio did not want to offend or alienate any of its white audience, hence they edited the film in a way that de-emphasizes certain racist behaviors of whites.

The 1961 film version of *A Raisin in the Sun* won an award at the Cannes Film Festival and was hailed by critics as a worthy cinematic version of the stage play which won the 1959 New York Drama Critics Circle Award. Lorraine Hansberry was pleased with the result. In an article in the *New York Herald Tribune,* she wrote: "The film which I have finally seen is to me, at least, an extraordinary one. Everywhere in its texture is the devotion and creativity of the gifted cast and of two men: its initial guardian, Philip Rose, and director Dan Petrie." Hansberry went on to praise Mr. Petrie's "sensitivity . . . and completely successful respect for the *unities of drama* as applied to film" [emphasis added]. Although she concluded that "the result is a thing of beauty," she felt compelled to refer to her original filmscripts (there were two previous versions) in which she abandoned the classical "unities of drama" for a more sweeping vision. "Born to the romance of the [poet Carl] Sandburg image of the great city's landscape, I was excited by the opportunity to deal with it visually and sent the formerly housebound characters hither and yon into the city." Most of that location footage ended up on the floor of the cutting room, she states, because her uncut version resulted in over three hours of film.

With the publication of this [the unfilmed screenplay], readers will not only realize the scope of her cinematic vision for the play but will discover that far more than time was cut from the script. A close reading of the *Herald Tribune* article by Hansberry suggests she was being somewhat careful to praise Petrie's ability to film essentially the stage drama, not unlike the achievements of good television filming of stage plays. And although she was apparently pleased with "what he has composed, with genuine pictorial sweep, . . . the rise and fall of the arc of the drama through a stunning filmic eye," the result represented a choice different from her original conception.

It is worth noting that, while critics praised the film for bringing the stage play to millions of viewers and for preserving its fine dramatic qualities—the latter in large part the achievement of the stellar cast who had originated the roles in the Broadway production—most noted that the play remained essentially intact except for a few scenes set outside the confines of the Younger home. . . .

## THE YOUNGERS IN THE OUTSIDE WORLD

Hansberry's cinematic vision was indeed of Sandburgian sweep as she sought to make her characters quintessential Chicagoans. She wanted to widen the camera's view beyond the cramped Younger apartment to encompass the "City of the Big Shoulders" and its contradictions. The vast financial opportunities and attractive housing of that metropolis are not available to the Youngers, despite their generations of hard work to support the affluent lifestyle of Chicago's privileged. Hansberry, a master of words, willingly sacrificed some of the brilliant dialogue of her stage drama for the eloquence of the visual image. The opening shot was to pan the city landscape of the Southside, the "Negro" part of town, with its overcrowded neighborhoods, children playing in the street for want of a safer playground, and boulevards peopled by the unemployed and the underemployed. In an effective use of the written word as if spoken, she imposes Langston Hughes's poem "Harlem," which inspired the title of the work, one line at a time, over the panning shots. Because the poem is an extended question ("What happens to a dream deferred? Does it . . . ?"), this projection of the text as image immediately engages the viewer to "ask" the question that frames the film's thesis. The final phrase, *"Or does it explode?"* hangs over the Southside images as both promise and threat.

The opening scene of her unfilmed script retains aspects so familiar to this play—the family slowly rising for the day, the simmering quarrel between Walter and Ruth, the warm moments with Travis, their son, the humor of Beneatha as she counters Walter's criticisms, and finally, the appearance of Lena Younger, family matriarch. After this introduction of the primary characters, and a brief screen moment for Lena, Hansberry's camera focuses on Lena's hands, an image that will be used in the next scenes to "tell" the work history of Lena and women like her: her hands carefully buttoning up the coat of a little girl, the daughter of the white couple for whom she works; her hands immersed in soap suds, washing the child's favorite toy; the sparkling kitchen rendered spotless by her hands. Lena's hands are the hands of the countless laborers who have scrubbed floors, polished silver, combed hair, fixed meals, and in the case of men, dug trenches for railroad ties, built bridges, and chauffeured cars so that Chicago and other cities like it could boast their high standards of living. Through this image, Hansberry connects Lena's work to that of her son, Walter. However, Walter's hands are shown buttoning up his livery coat, while superimposed are images of the lush home of his employer and the district in which he lives, the privileged wife with manicured, jeweled hands, and a garage "itself more fit for human habitation." Walter's hands grip a steering wheel or rest idly and impatiently on the dashboard; he is no closer to his family's dreams of opportunity and progress than is his mother. He, too, is part of a domestic staff, with no better-paying job in his future.

Later, as Lena and Walter return home on streetcar or bus from different parts of the city, the camera follows their eyes as each sees the object of their dreams: Lena, a modest, attractive house in a quiet, middle-class neighborhood; Walter, a successful liquor store near his home. Again, the camera pans the neighborhoods, striking a sharp contrast between the places where the Youngers work and where they live. The camera finds Beneatha in the student lounge of the university that she attends, learning Yoruban words from Asagai, her Nigerian friend. Beneatha's concerns about financing her college education offer a counterpoint to the comfort implicit in these surroundings which display the relative leisure of student life (the time to study, to ponder, and to relax).

Before reaching home, Lena stops to buy some apples at a local Southside market, but is angered by a flippant and disrespectful white clerk as well as the poor quality and high price of fruit that, as she says, "was at the Last Supper!" She takes a long bus detour out to the open markets of the far Southside, a Chicago landmark "where the world's finest produce is exhibited for blocks and blocks in the open air," and buys voluptuous apples for a more reasonable price. The economic exploitation of the impoverished Black neighborhoods, seemingly a permanent fixture in urban life, is inescapable in this segment.

Before arriving home, Walter has his own encounter with an unconscious agent of racism when he stops off at Herman's Liquors to ask the owner about the liquor business, and his own interest in investing in a liquor store. In this remarkable scene, Hansberry reveals "the irony of noncommunication between the two men." She writes, in her directorial notes, that "there is nothing 'racist' in Herman's attitude to Walter." He means to be helpful and genuine, but the men are separated by decades of discrimination and deferred dreams. Herman lapses into the typical shopkeeper's complaint about long hours, spendthrift wife, and general hardship. He does not understand that Walter, who has never owned anything much in his life, would welcome such problems so that he could be his own boss and provide for his family as Herman does. Walter, offended by Herman's patronizing attitude, abruptly walks out. The next time Walter is seen on screen, he is drinking with

Willy and Bobo, plotting to get part of the insurance money for their investment.

## THE USE OF MONTAGE

The next scenes move to the Younger interior and include the marvelous moments, though somewhat edited, immortalized by the stage play: the arrival of the $10,000 check, the discovery that Ruth is pregnant and has made a down payment for an abortion, Lena's rejection of Walter's investment proposal, Beneatha's modeling of Asagai's gift and her attempt to dance "African," Walter's angry encounter with George Murchison (Beneatha's date and a personification of bourgeois values), and finally, Lena's revelation that she has used the insurance money to make a down payment on a house for the family.

Walter's disappointment and frustration with his mother's decision are heightened for the viewer by a montage of shots of Walter drinking alone, driving out of the city to the marshlands bordering Lake Calumet, looking at the great steel mills of South Chicago, perusing the stockyards, wandering aimlessly in the downtown Loop amidst the midday crowd, and finally sitting on a curb in the shadow of the Negro Soldier's monument on the Southside. This panorama of possibility, hope, and accomplishment ends with perhaps the most poignant and ironic symbol of African American history and achievement: a monument to men who fought bravely on foreign soil for their country only to be denied at home a share of their nation's promise.

Hansberry's script immediately crystallizes this visual montage in the brilliant street orator scene. Walter wanders onto a street meeting where a middle-aged man in a tired business suit and tie addresses a growing crowd of black people, mostly men. With great sarcasm and to the delight of the crowd, he characterizes their experience—coming from the South to Chicago, "the Promised Land," seeking something better than Mississippi, Georgia, and other Jim Crow states offered, only to be handed a mop and a broom by "the very man who has stolen his homeland, put him in bondage, defamed his nation, robbed him of his heritage!" He compares black Americans to blacks in Africa who are standing up for their rights to self-determination and then asks, "How much has to happen before the black man in the United States is going to understand that God helps those who help themselves? . . . We are the only people in the world who own nothing, who make nothing! . . . Where are your textile or steel mills? Heh? Where are your mighty houses of finance?" In a nice touch, Hansberry places both Asagai, Beneatha's Nigerian friend, and Walter, who have not yet met each other, in the crowd—each with his own reaction. This segment relieves Walter of pleading his own case, as he must during most of the original play and the 1961 film. Walter's frustration is identified with that of many (especially Black men), as the viewers see for themselves the source of Walter's anger and hear from the street orator the harsh sounds of a deferred dream about to explode.

With this prelude, the viewer can readily understand Walter's euphoria when Lena decides to release to him (and his judgment) the balance of the insurance money. That this scene takes place at a dance given by George Murchison's fraternity and attended by Walter and Ruth stretches credi-

---

### HANSBERRY AND BLACK CINEMA

*Filmmaker Spike Lee acknowledges the greatness of the play and the film of* Raisin, *but he believes that Hansberry's unfilmed screenplay could have been the basis of a landmark in cinema, as the play had been a landmark in American theater. In terms of Hansberry's significance in African American culture and history, Lee puts her in the company of Martin Luther King Jr. and Malcolm X.*

*History* is an important word, an important concept, but today it seems like this particular word is foreign to a lot of us African Americans. The history I'm talking about is not ancient African history either; it's recent history. . . . Young African American kids know the names of Martin Luther King, Jr., and Malcolm X, but it's a very superficial knowledge. A lot of us are again clueless about Ms. Hansberry.

It's time to include Lorraine Hansberry in those history lessons. Reading her original screenplay of *A Raisin in the Sun* was a revelation for me. I had seen the movie on television, but I was too young to have seen the Broadway production (I would have probably liked it better than the film). Like all great works of art, this stuff doesn't get old. And for me *Raisin* is still fresh, it's still relevant. Lorraine Hansberry was a visionary.

Today, everybody and their mother are talking about "Afrocentricity." But Hansberry was writing about it long before it became fashionable. ("Hell no, don't call me no African! I'm a

bility, since such behavior seems totally out of character for Walter. However, it does suggest some of the bourgeois pretensions implicit in Walter's desires and foreshadows the disappointment to come.

## RACISM, OVERT AND COVERT

In another significant foray outside the Younger apartment, the family visits the new house and neighborhood into which they plan to move. Although a similar trip was included in the 1961 film, Hansberry's original directions included a panning shot of the surrounding houses which revealed "something sinister. . . . At some windows curtains drop quickly back into place as though those who are watching do not want to be seen; at others—shadowy figures simply move back out of view when they feel that Walter and Ruth's gaze is upon them; at still others, those who are staring do so without apology. The faces, the eyes of women and

Negro, I'm colored, etc., etc." We've all heard that numerous times.) For me, the brilliance of *Raisin* is the examination of the African American family. . . .

But with this recent so-called "explosion" of black cinema, the names most repeated are Oscar Micheaux, Gordon Parks, Ossie Davis, and Melvin Van Peebles. From this day on, I'm going to start to include Ms. Hansberry. Her play is a landmark in American theater, and in the right hands, the film could have been a landmark in cinema. (Regardless, it still stands as an important piece.) One sees the freedom she had with the play that Hollywood, or in this specific case, Columbia Pictures, wasn't having.

After I finished reading the screenplay, I went out and rented the video cassette. It seems to me all the cuts had to deal with softening a too defiant black voice. I found the parts that were cut to be some of the most interesting parts of the screenplay. . . .

You might ask, what would Hansberry have done if she hadn't been taken away from us so soon? I'd like to think that *Raisin* would have been her first of many fine screenplays. Can you name another African American female who has written a screenplay for a Hollywood studio that got made? I cannot.

Spike Lee, "Commentary: Thoughts on the Screenplay," in A Raisin in the Sun, *The Unfilmed Original Screenplay*, Robert Nemiroff, ed. New York: Plume/Penguin, 1992, pp. xlv–xlvii.

children, in the main, look hard with a curiosity that, for the most part, is clearly hostile." This brief visual moment emphasizes the dangers awaiting the Youngers in their new neighborhood and the courage of their decision to move.

By taking the camera outside the Younger apartment in her script and following the adult characters in their normal daily lives, Hansberry forces her audience to see the conditions and circumstances that drive a man like Walter to strike out at his family, that motivated Walter's father to quite literally work himself to death, that led Ruth to risk abortion rather than add another child to the family, and that impel a Lena Younger to move into a hostile neighborhood. The camera's eye would be irrefutable as it swept the panorama of Chicago and, by implication, America's major cities where the majority of African Americans reside.

Hansberry also accomplishes something else which the structure of the stage play and the 1961 film version could not—revealing the many subtle ways in which racism invades the characters' lives on a daily basis. The early scene with Mrs. Holiday, the woman for whom Lena works, is a case in point. It is a fascinating study in the complexities of the relationship between domestic and employer. On the one hand, Lena is gentle, though lovingly gruff and demanding, with the Holiday child on this, her last day before retirement. When Mrs. Holiday questions by mere tone of voice whether Lena can really say good-bye to the child—suggesting in that moment the historic myth that mammies surely prefer their white charges over their own families—Lena curtly affirms that the good-bye is indeed a final one.

Lena remains unmoved even when Mrs. Holiday indicates that her leaving will cause some "hardship" for the family, since she will probably have to stop working until she can find a suitable replacement. When Mrs. Holiday finally accepts the inevitable, Lena relaxes and speaks in a more friendly and intimate tone, telling her about her work history, first for a woman who considered her "part of the family" and used that as an excuse to severely underpay her, and later Lena's failed attempt to retrain for employment in the defense industry. She speaks with pride of her husband, who mastered the new demands of defense employment and left his porter job for good. This dimension of Lena, who could easily be portrayed as a stereotypical mammy if not handled with sensitivity, allows the viewer to understand her insistence on certain values and the significance of the insurance money to her and her family. Without this scene, we fail to comprehend fully Lena Younger and the years of Mrs. Holidays and worse that she has lived through. Scenes like this lend texture to the lives of the Younger family.

## CUTS FOR POLITICAL AND COMMERCIAL REASONS

Why were such important scenes cut from the film that was made? In my opinion, the editing of Hansberry's film script was implicitly political and began with the editorial notes of production director Samuel Briskin (secured sometime later by Robert Nemiroff, Hansberry's literary executor). It is a measure of the cultural ignorance of the times that Briskin registered confusion at the pet names used by the family— that Beneatha was called "Bennie," and Walter Lee "Brother." "Jive" expressions, such as "Man," "I mean," and "like," were deleted as much as possible. These and other colloquialisms were essentially purged from the script.

Other comments and recommendations were more insidious, such as deleting the white clerk who was fresh to Lena in the market, cutting the scene in Herman's liquor store after registering a failure to understand why Walter gets angry at the store owner, questioning the play's explicit references to colonialism perpetrated by the British and the French, and questioning the advisability of most racial references such as "white boys." Also cut from the script was a brief reference to the quality of Travis's school. His teacher asks him and his classmates to bring fifty cents for a fund to buy special books "that tell all about the things the poor Negroes did." The issue of teaching "Negro history" as something different and apart (probably during a one-week "celebration") and the teacher's constant reference to "poor Negroes" get lost in the more urgent money problems of the family. But the comments quickly remind us that quality of education is another reason that families like the Youngers move to other neighborhoods.

Briskin circled "white— black—" in Asagai's speech referring to the white and black women that he had known and probably dated. Beneatha's blasphemous speech about God raised the question, "Are we apt to get church criticism on this?" And, in an amusing example of illiteracy, Briskin suggested that Beneatha's speech to George about the "Ashanti performing surgical operations when the British were still tattooing themselves with blue dragons" be replaced by suggesting that the "Americans were doing something or other." Obviously, at that time, the only Americans were Native Americans.

Briskin speaks with the voice and authority of the movie studios (Columbia in this instance), who were incredibly cautious about offending the American (i.e., white) public. This timidity is most evident in the deletion of Hansberry's new scenes depicting encounters with whites, in particular, Lena's scene with Mrs. Holiday and Walter's meeting with the liquor store owner. Neither white character is blatantly racist, but rather displays that persistent insensitivity and often willful blindness that cuts as deeply as, but less conspicuously than, legal segregation. The subtle racism of the North is Hansberry's target. These characters are not the "white other," the Southern bigot whose outrageous actions are easily distanced, but resemble more closely probably those whom the studio hoped to attract to the film. Only the scenes with Lindner, message-carrier for the Clyborne Park Association, were retained. Tested in the highly successful stage production, they were clearly regarded as safe.

The fear of what Hollywood would do with her film had made Hansberry very reluctant to sell the movie rights. "My twenty years of memory of Hollywood treatment of 'Negro materials,'" she wrote in her newspaper article, "plus the more commonly decried aspects of Hollywood tradition, led me to visualize slit skirts and rolling eyeballs, with the latest nightclub singer playing the family's college daughter. I did not feel it was my right or duty to help present the American public with yet another later-day [*sic*] minstrel show." Yet despite the ignorance and timidity expressed by the production director, Hansberry apparently felt that the final script met her high standard for socially responsible art, and retained the essential spirit, dignity, and quality of the original play which, she said, had gone up on Broadway "without a single line having been changed for the 'buyers' or anyone else."

## HANSBERRY'S INSTINCTS CORRECT

Daniel Petrie, director of the 1961 film, was not so sanguine about the results after seeing his work at the Cannes Film Festival. He was quite disappointed with the European reception of the film, which received a special Gary Cooper Award for "human values" but was bypassed for Cannes' regular prizes. "Objections to *A Raisin in the Sun* . . . mentioned the excessive dialogue—all too literally translated in three-layer subtitles—and the confinement of the action to the stage set without moving outdoors. Also, while the theme was liked, there was so little visual emphasis on the poor living conditions of the Chicago Negro family that foreign audiences didn't see what they had to complain about."

Petrie concluded that the final cutting of the film was at fault. The exterior scenes in the original screenplay, which were filmed on location in Chicago and visually depicted the crucial housing problems of the city, extended the length of the film to two hours and forty minutes. "To shorten it," commented Petrie, "most of the visual description of the neighborhood was removed, while almost all of the play's dialogue remained. When I saw the foreign audience grow restless, I was convinced that the wrong things had been cut out." Hansberry's initial cinematic instincts were on the mark. Her exterior scenes, which included the family's encounters with the dominant and oppressive culture, documented the conditions that drove the characters in her play and provided the context for any audience to understand the dilemma and frustration of the Younger family.

## WHICH CHARACTER IS THE LEAD?

In the original film script, Hansberry may have attempted to correct what she considered to be a flaw in the stage drama. She wrote: "Fine plays tend to utilize one big fat character who runs right through the middle of the structure, by action or implication, with whom we rise or fall. A central character as such is certainly lacking from *Raisin*. . . . The result is that neither Walter Lee nor Mama Younger loom [*sic*] large enough to monumentally command the play. I consider it an enormous dramatic fault if no one else does. . . ." This dual protagonist structure set the stage for the struggle for primacy between actors Sidney Poitier and Claudia McNeil in the 1959 Broadway production. The audience's recognition of the matriarchal figure as portrayed by a powerful McNeil and the culturally conditioned fear of the volatile Walter tended to award the victory to Lena.

Without making major revisions in the play for her screenplay, Hansberry subtly tilts the balance toward Walter Lee from Lena Younger by emphasizing Walter's role as a representative of African American men. She drops the warrior scene in which Beneatha and Walter dance to African rhythms and Walter, in a drunken speech to his "African brothers," speaks in another, more subliminal voice as he momentarily identifies with the proud, militant heritage of his forebears. That moment was delightful to those who viewed it as innocent play, but was problematic for others. It seemed completely out of character for Walter, who constantly denigrates Beneatha's identification with Africa. Because of Walter's drunken state, his speech tends to undercut any serious notions of brotherhood among people of African descent. Whatever the interpretation, Hansberry achieves much more with the street orator who, speaking for Walter, connects unequivocally the struggle of African Americans to that of Africans with very explicit and compelling arguments. Hansberry insists that the crowd at the street meeting be primarily male, thereby emphasizing the particularly insidious effects of racism and discrimination on the African American male. Bringing gender into the foreground in this way helps to frame Walter's sexist remarks about the women in his family who "man the barricades," who have "small minds," and who generally prevent him (and men like him) from taking the bold actions he believes are necessary to be successful in this country.

Hansberry also clarifies the motivation for Walter's decision to reject Lindner's offer in the final moments of the film. There has been much debate as to the reasons for his change of heart. Is it the overpowering presence and pressure of his mother, who insists that his son be present, that shames Walter into changing his mind? Or is it something inside Walter that insists on the more prideful choice? The answer determines Walter's stature as either a man dragged kicking and screaming into his mother's definition of manhood or a man who is capable of a courageous and rather stunning act of self-realization. Hansberry leaves no doubt as to her intentions.

> WALTER: What's the matter with you all? I didn't make this world! It was give to me this way! Hell yes (*to his sister*) I want me some yachts someday! Yes, I want to hang some real pearls round my wife's neck! Ain't she supposed to wear no pearls? Somebody tell me *who* it is who decides which women is supposed to wear pearls in this world? I tell you, I am a *man*—and I think my wife should wear some pearls in this world!
>
> . . . *The last line hangs and Walter begins to move about the room with enormous agitation, as if the word "man" has set off its own reaction in his mind. He mumbles it to himself as*

*he moves about.* **The interplay of his conflict is at work now in him, no matter what he says. It is the realization that begins now that will decide his actions to come; thus he is quarreling with Walter Lee; all actions he performs are to persuade himself.** [Emphasis added]

## TWO DIFFERENT ENDINGS

Finally, Hansberry makes a subtle but telling change in the ending of the screenplay. In the original drama, Mama is left alone on the stage, after the family members have exited with the last of their belongings.

*For a long, long moment, she looks around and up and out at all the walls and ceilings, crosses Upstage Right to what was once her and Big Walter's bedroom, touches the door jamb, crosses Centerstage and suddenly, despite her, a great heaving thing rises in her and she puts her fist to her mouth to stifle it, takes a final desperate look, pulls her coat about her, pats her hat and exits.—The lights come down even more—and she comes back in, grabs her plant, and goes out for the last time. Lights down and out.*

FINAL CURTAIN

In contrast, the screenplay ends with *both* Walter and Lena in the frame.

WALTER: (*gently*) Mama, why don't you come on!

LENA: I'm coming, I'm coming.

WALTER: (*grinning to relieve the moment*) Mama, how we gonna pay for this house?

LENA: Well, I was just thinking the other day that I didn't like not working much as I thought I did. . . . I guess I call Mrs. Holiday in the morning—see if they got somebody else yet. . . .

*They suddenly look at each other in a flash of remembrance, and Walter turns and goes to the window and gets the plant and comes back and puts it in his mother's hands, and they go out and down the steps—their conversation about the nature of the future going on: Walter suggesting that Charlie Atkins might someday want a partner if he can get the capital together. . . .*

FADE OUT

Both endings are preceded by the comments by Lena and Ruth that Walter has come into his manhood, but the latter scene emphasizes Walter's new role in the family as co-leader with his mother. The plant, which "expresses" Lena, remains a critical symbol here. It embodies her hopes, dreams and values. The fact that Lena *and* Walter suddenly "remember" it and that Walter places the plant in her hands is poignant affirmation that Walter has indeed accepted those human principles that have seen his family through generations of discrimination. At the same time, he represents a new generation of African Americans who will and must seek their future in the opportunities offered by their own times. In these post-feminist 1990s, such a change may achieve Hansberry's intention to emphasize the plight of Walter more effectively. In the earlier versions, Walter Lee often seems infantile in his actions, and his reactions read as tantrums in a world sensitized to feminist issues. Combined with the location shots that emphasize the economic and social traps surrounding him, this change in the ending grants him greater stature without sacrificing the central importance of Lena.

# The 1973 Musical Is Better than the Play

Clive Barnes

Clive Barnes is a longtime theater critic who succeeded reviewer Brooks Atkinson at the *New York
Times*. Calling the musical version of *Raisin* "a
strange one but a good one," he praises both the
adaptation by Robert Nemiroff and Charlotte
Zaltzberg and the "tremendous story" that remained
relevant years after its original publication. Barnes
found the material so effectively developed that, with
all due respect to Hansberry, he considers it "slightly
firmer and better" than the original.

Broadway last night got its first new musical of the season.
It is a strange one but a good one, it warms the heart and
touches the soul. The musical is "Raisin," and it has come to
Broadway via Washington's Arena Stage. It is based on the
late Lorraine Hansberry's 1959 watershed of a play "A Raisin
in the Sun."

Miss Hansberry's play about a working-class black family
in Chicago aspiring to move into a white suburb was full of
guts and sentiment. It was an immeasurably moving if oc-
casionally diffuse play. Why then make it into a musical?

Well, one good reason might be that the present book by
Robert Nemiroff and Charlotte Zaltzberg is perhaps even
better than the play. It retains all of Miss Hansberry's finest
dramatic encounters, with the dialogue, as cutting and as
honest as ever, intact. But the shaping of the piece is slightly
firmer and better. The characters are still as large and as
likely as life.

## HEROISM THROUGH OPPRESSION

The play has an oddly period flavor now. Racial situations
have perhaps not changed as much as we would like to

Reprinted from Clive Barnes, "*Raisin* in Musical Form," *The New York Times*, May 31,
1973, with permission. Copyright © 1973 by The New York Times.

think. One wonders how welcome a black family would find itself on Park Avenue—or, nowadays, a white family in better-class black neighborhoods. But "Raisin" is early Martin Luther King, when the N.A.A.C.P. was a growing force in the land. Indeed a time when blacks were either Negro, colored or ignored.

Today it is not the color of the piece that overwhelms one but its tremendous story, and its touching picture of a family fighting for life. The big momma, the wayward son and his loving wife, the pert kid sister and unconcerned little grandchild, this is a family that could be almost anywhere at any time. You only need oppression to bring out the tragedy and heroism in people.

## MUSIC IS SECONDARY

In a sense the score (music by Judd Wolden and lyrics by Robert Brittan) for "Raisin" is not the most important aspect of the show. There are some good ballad and gospel numbers, a striking revival meeting scene, an African love song and some lively dance numbers—but it is not a score of any considerable power and originality.

You hardly notice this—or at least you only notice it in passing—not only because of the exceptionally superior book, but also the enormous strength of the staging and the performance. Both are faultless.

## "THEY HAVE PULLED IT OFF"

When "Raisin" was first given by the Arena Stage in Washington this spring I was most enthusiastic about Donald McKayle's fluent and simple staging and the toughly personal performances of the cast. Yet, I was a shade dubious about its Broadway production. The Arena Stage is comparatively small and I feared some loss of intimacy. Moreover, the Arena Stage is a theater completely in the round, and Mr. McKayle's dazzling production made the most of it, as did Robert U. Taylor's purposely bland yet subtly evocative settings.

Well, they have pulled it off. Mr. McKayle has opened up his staging to its advantage. The dance numbers rank among the best in years. Like Jerome Robbins, Mr. McKayle comes to the musical theater as a ranking choreographer, but also like Mr. Robbins his skill with actors must now be unquestioned.

Imaginatively and meaningful, this brings the pure magic of calculated simplicity to the musical theater, and Mr. Taylor's tenement townscape serves equally well as a background for ghetto, bar, chapel or house, while Bernard Johnson's costumes had a neatly nineteen-fifties look to them.

## EXCELLENT ACTING

The performances blaze—not just one, or two, but every single one of them. As the Mama, Virginia Capers, a vast and loving Gibraltar of a woman, was tremendous in just about every sense you can use the word. But her almost overpowering matriarch was matched by the rest.

The son, Joe Morton, sang with passion and had just the right mixture of foolishness, ambition and decency; Ernestine Jackson was beautiful, womanly and appealing as the wife; Helen Martin made an attractively acidulated neighbor; Deborah Allen proved spirited and witty as the kid sister; and Robert Jackson charmed as her Nigerian boyfriend.

Finally, there is that mighty little atom of a child star, Ralph Carter, who gives cuteness a new dimension of decency, and might well be the kind of child actor even W.C. Fields could grow to love.

The chorus was outstanding and the dancing had an energy and grace rarely seen on Broadway these days. "Raisin" is one of those unusual musicals that should not only delight people who love musicals, but might also well delight people who don't. It is a show with a heartbeat very much of its own.

# The 1989 Video Revival and the Restored Scenes

Robert Nemiroff

Robert Nemiroff was eminently qualified to write about *A Raisin in the Sun* not only because he was married to Lorraine Hansberry at the time it was written but also because he was her frequent writing collaborator. He produced and/or adapted many of her works and won the Tony Award in 1974 for his adaptation of the musical *Raisin.* In 1988, twenty-three years after Hansberry's death, Nemiroff wrote a new introduction for the book, from which this selection is taken.

Also in 1988, the American Playhouse did a revival of the play for television and video, which featured Danny Glover as Walter Younger and Esther Rolle as Mama. As Nemiroff discusses here, some scenes were cut from the original play in order to quicken its pace and keep the running time down. None of the cuts, he says, prevent *Raisin* from being a great play; however, their significance to the overall sense of the play cannot be overstated. Since the original play, many scenes have been partially or completely restored.

This [1988 edition] is the most complete edition of *A Raisin in the Sun* ever published. Like the American Playhouse production for television, it restores to the play two scenes unknown to the general public, and a number of other key scenes and passages staged for the first time in twenty-fifth anniversary revivals and, most notably, the Roundabout Theatre's Kennedy Center production on which the television picture is based.

"The events of every passing year add resonance to *A Raisin in the Sun.* It is as if history is conspiring to make the

Excerpted from the Introduction, by Robert Nemiroff, copyright © 1987, 1988 by Robert Nemiroff, to *A Raisin in the Sun*, by Lorraine Hansberry. Used by permission of Dutton Signet, a division of Penguin Putnam Inc.

play a classic"; ". . . one of a handful of great American dramas . . . *A Raisin in the Sun* belongs in the inner circle, along with *Death of a Salesman, Long Day's Journey into Night,* and *The Glass Menagerie.*" So wrote the *New York Times* and the *Washington Post* respectively of Harold Scott's revelatory stagings for the Roundabout in which most of these elements, cut on Broadway, were restored. The unprecedented resurgence of the work (a dozen regional revivals at this writing, new publications and productions abroad, and now the television production that will be seen by millions) prompts the new edition.

## R*AISIN* AS P*ROPHECY*

Produced in 1959, the play presaged the revolution in black and women's consciousness—and the revolutionary ferment in Africa—that exploded in the years following the playwright's death in 1965 to ineradicably alter the social fabric and consciousness of the nation and the world. As so many have commented lately, it did so in a manner and to an extent that few could have foreseen, for not only the restored material, but much else that passed unnoticed in the play at the time, speaks to issues that are now inescapable: value systems of the black family; concepts of African American beauty and identity; class and generational conflicts; the relationships of husbands and wives, black men and women; the outspoken (if then yet unnamed) feminism of the daughter; and, in the penultimate scene between Beneatha and Asagai, the larger statement of the play—and the ongoing struggle it portends.

## M*ATERIAL* T*HAT* N*EVER* M*ADE* I*T TO THE* S*TAGE*

Not one of the cuts, it should be emphasized, was made to dilute or censor the play or to "soften" its statement, for everyone in that herculean, now-legendary band that brought *Raisin* to Broadway—and most specifically the producer, Philip Rose, and director, Lloyd Richards—*believed* in the importance of that statement with a degree of commitment that would have countenanced nothing of the kind. How and why, then, did the cuts come about?

The scene in which Beneatha unveils her natural haircut is an interesting example. In 1959, when the play was presented, the rich variety of Afro styles introduced in the mid-sixties had not yet arrived: the very few black women who wore their hair unstraightened cut it very short. When the hair of Diana Sands (who created the role) was cropped in this fashion, however, a few days before the opening, it was not contoured to suit her: her particular facial structure required a fuller Afro, of the sort she in fact adopted in later years. Result? Rather than vitiate the playwright's point—the beauty of black hair—the scene was dropped.

### RUNNING TIME AND FINDING A CO-PRODUCER

Some cuts were similarly the result of happenstance or unpredictables of the kind that occur in any production: difficulties with a scene, the "processes" of actors, the dynamics of staging, etc. But most were related to the length of the play: running time. Time in the context of bringing to Broadway the first play by a black (young and unknown) woman, to be directed, moreover, by another unknown black "first," in a theater where black audiences virtually did not exist—and where, in the entire history of the American stage, there had never been a serious *commercially successful* black drama!

So unlikely did the prospects seem in that day, in fact, to all but Phil Rose and the company, that much as some expressed admiration for the play, Rose's eighteen-month effort to find a co-producer to help complete the financing was turned down by virtually every established name in the business. He was joined at the last by another newcomer, David Cogan, but even with the money in hand, not a single theater owner on the Great White Way would *rent* to the new production! So that when the play left New York for tryouts—with a six-hundred-dollar advance in New Haven and no theater to come back to—had the script and performance been any less ready, and the response of critics and audiences any less unreserved than they proved to be, *A Raisin in the Sun* would never have reached Broadway.

Under these circumstances the pressures were enormous (if unspoken and rarely even acknowledged in the excitement of the work) *not* to press fate unduly with unnecessary risks. And the most obvious of these was the running time. It is one thing to present a four-and-a-half-hour drama by Eugene O'Neill on Broadway—but a *first* play (even ignoring the special features of this one) in the neighborhood of even *three*??? By common consensus, the need to keep the show as tight and streamlined as possible was manifest. Some things—philosophical flights, nuances the general audience might not understand, shadings, embellishments—would have to be sacrificed.

## MAMA KIDNAPPED BY WHITE AMERICA

At the time the cuts were made (there were also some very good ones that focused and strengthened the drama), it was assumed by all that they would in no way significantly affect or alter the statement of the play, for there is nothing in the omitted lines that is not implicit elsewhere, and throughout, *A Raisin in the Sun.* But to think this was to reckon without two factors the future would bring into play. The first was the swiftness and depth of the revolution in consciousness that was coming and the consequent, perhaps inevitable, tendency of some people to assume, because the "world" had changed, that any "successful" work which preceded the change must embody the values they had outgrown. And the second was the nature of the American audience.

James Baldwin has written that "Americans suffer from an ignorance that is not only colossal, but sacred." He is referring to that apparently endless capacity we have nurtured through long years to deceive ourselves where race is concerned: the baggage of myth and preconception we carry with us that enables northerners, for example, to shield themselves from the extent and virulence of segregation in the North, so that each time an "incident" of violence so egregious that they cannot look past it occurs they are "shocked" anew, as if it had never happened before or as if the problem were largely passé. . . .

But Baldwin is referring also to the human capacity, where a work of art is involved, to substitute, for what the writer has written, what in our hearts we *wish* to believe. As Hansberry put it in response to one reviewer's enthusiastic, if particularly misguided praise of her play: ". . . it did not disturb the writer in the least that there is no such implication in the entire three acts. He did not need it in the play; he had it in his head."

Such problems did not, needless to say, stop America from embracing *A Raisin in the Sun.* But it did interfere drastically, for a generation, with the way the play was interpreted and assessed—and, in hindsight, it made all the more regrettable the abridgment (though without it would we even know the play today?). In a remarkable rumination on Hansberry's death, Ossie Davis (who succeeded Sidney Poitier in the role of Walter Lee) put it this way:

> The play deserved all this—the playwright deserved all this, and more. Beyond question! But I have a feeling that for all she got, Lorraine Hansberry never got all she deserved in regard to *A Raisin in the Sun*—that she got success, but that in her success she was cheated, both as a writer and as a Negro.
>
> One of the biggest selling points about *Raisin*—filling the grapevine, riding the word-of-mouth, laying the foundation for its wide, wide acceptance—was how much the Younger family was just like any other American family. Some people were ecstatic to find that "it didn't really have to be about Negroes at all!" It was, rather, a walking, talking, living demonstration of our mythic conviction that, underneath, all of us Americans, *color-ain't-got-nothing-to-do-with-it*, are pretty much alike. People are just people, whoever they are; and all they want is a chance to be like other people. This uncritical assumption, sentimentally held by the audience, powerfully fixed in the character of the powerful mother with whom everybody could identify, immediately and completely, made any other questions about the Youngers, and what living in the slums of Southside Chicago had done to them, not only irrelevant and impertinent, but also disloyal . . . because everybody who walked into the theater saw in Lena Younger . . . his own great American Mama. And that was decisive.

In effect, as Davis went on to develop, white America "kidnapped" Mama, stole her away and used her fantasized image to avoid what was uniquely *African* American in the play. And what it was saying.

Thus, in many reviews (and later academic studies), the Younger family—maintained by two female domestics and a chauffeur, son of a laborer dead of a lifetime of hard labor—was transformed into an acceptably "middle class" family. The decision to move became a desire to "integrate" (rather than, as Mama says simply, "to find the nicest house for the least amount of money for my family. . . . Them houses they put up for colored in them areas way out always seem to cost twice as much."). . . .

Mama herself—about whose "acceptance" of her "place" in the society there is not a word in the play, and who, in quest of her family's survival over the soul- and body-crushing conditions of the ghetto, is prepared to defy housing-pattern taboos, threats, bombs, and God knows what else—became the safely "conservative" matriarch, upholder of the social order and proof that if one only perseveres with faith, everything will come out right in the end and the-system-ain't-so-bad-after-all. (All this, presumably, because, true to character, she speaks and thinks in the *language* of her generation, shares their dream of a better life and, like millions of her counterparts, takes her Christianity to heart.) At the same time, necessarily, Big Walter Younger—the husband who reared this family with her and whose unseen presence and influence can be heard in every scene—vanished from analysis.

And perhaps most ironical of all to the playwright, who had herself as a child been almost killed in such a real-life story, the climax of the play became, pure and simple, a "happy ending"—despite the fact that it leaves the Youngers on the brink of what will surely be, in their new home, at *best* a nightmare of uncertainty. ("If he thinks that's a happy ending," said Hansberry in an interview, "I invite him to come live in one of the communities where the Youngers are going!") Which is not even to mention the fact that that little house in a blue-collar neighborhood—hardly suburbia, as some have imagined—is hardly the answer to the deeper needs and inequities of race and class and sex that Walter and Beneatha have articulated.

## RESTORING SOME BUT NOT ALL CUTS

When Lorraine Hansberry read the reviews—delighted by the accolades, grateful for the recognition, but also deeply troubled—she decided in short order to put back many of the materials excised. She did that in the 1959 Random House edition, but faced with the actuality of a prize-winning play, she hesitated about some others which, for reasons now beside the point, had not in rehearsal come alive. She later felt, however, that the full last scene between Beneatha and Asagai (drastically cut on Broadway) and Walter's bedtime scene with Travis (eliminated entirely) should be restored at the first opportunity, and this was done in the 1966 New American Library edition. As anyone who has seen the recent productions will attest, they are among the most moving (and most applauded) moments in the play.

Because the visit of Mrs. Johnson adds the costs of another character to the cast and ten more minutes to the play, it has not been used in most revivals. But where it has been tried it has worked to solid—often hilarious—effect. It can be seen in the American Playhouse production, and is included here in any case, because it speaks to fundamental issues of the play, makes plain the reality that awaits the Youngers at the curtain, and, above all, makes clear what, in the eyes of the author, Lena Younger—in her typicality within the black experience—does and does *not* represent.

Another scene—the Act I, Scene Two moment in which Beneatha observes and Travis gleefully recounts his latest adventure in the street below—makes tangible and visceral one of the many facts of ghetto life that impel the Youngers' move. As captured on television and published here for the first time, it is its own sobering comment on just how "middle class" a family this is. . . .

## A "RECONCEIVED" PLAY

Finally, a note about the American Playhouse production. Unlike the drastically cut and largely one-dimensional 1961 movie version—which, affecting and pioneering though it may have been, reflected little of the greatness of the original stage performances—this new screen version is a luminous embodiment of the stage play as reconceived, but not altered, for the camera, and is exquisitely performed. That it is, is due inextricably to producer Chiz Schultz's and director Bill Duke's unswerving commitment to the text; Harold Scott's formative work with the stage company; Duke's own fresh insights and the cinematic brilliance of his reconception and direction for the screen; and the energizing infusion into this mix of Danny Glover's classic performance as Walter Lee to Esther Rolle's superlative Mama. As in the case of any production, I am apt to question a nuance here and there, and regrettably, because of a happenstance in production, the Walter-Travis scene has been omitted. But that scene will, I expect, be restored in the videocassette version of the picture. . . . It is thus an excellent version for study.

What is for me personally, as a witness to and sometime participant in the foregoing events, most gratifying about the current revival is that today, some twenty-nine years after Lorraine Hansberry, thinking back with disbelief a few nights after the opening of *Raisin*, typed out these words—

> . . . I had turned the last page out of the typewriter and pressed all the sheets neatly together in a pile, and gone and stretched out face down on the living room floor. I had finished a play; a play I had no reason to think or not think would ever be done; a play that I was sure no one would quite understand. . . .

—her play is not only being done, but that more than she had ever thought possible—and more clearly than it ever has been before—it is being "understood."

## *RAISIN* REMAINS FRESH

Yet one last point that I must make because it has come up so many times of late. I have been asked if I am not surprised that the play still remains so contemporary, and isn't that a "sad" commentary on America? It is indeed a sad commentary, but the question also assumes something more: that it is the topicality of the play's immediate events—i.e., the persistence of white opposition to unrestricted housing and the ugly manifestations of racism in its myriad forms—that keeps it alive. But I don't believe that such alone is what explains its vitality at all. For though the specifics of social mores and societal patterns will always change, the decline of the "New England territory" and the institution of the traveling salesman does not, for example, "date" *Death of a Salesman,* any more than the fact that we now recognize *love* (as opposed to interfamilial politics) as a legitimate basis for marriage obviates *Romeo and Juliet.* If we ever reach a time when the racial madness that afflicts America is at last truly behind us—as obviously *we must* if we are to survive in a world composed four-fifths of peoples of color—then I believe *A Raisin in the Sun* will remain no less pertinent. For at the deepest level it is not a specific situation but the human condition, human aspiration and human relationships—the persistence of dreams, of the bonds and conflicts between men and women, parents and children, old ways and new, and the endless struggle against human oppression, whatever the forms it may take, and for individual fulfillment, recognition, and liberation—that are at the heart of such plays. It is not surprising therefore that in each generation we recognize ourselves in them anew.

# CHRONOLOGY

**1930**

Lorraine Vivian Hansberry is born in Chicago, Illinois, on May 19.

**1938**

The Hansberry family moves into a white neighborhood near the University of Chicago; hostile residents protest and throw bricks; the family loses a lawsuit challenging segregated housing, is evicted after eight months' residence, and appeals case to federal courts.

**1940**

The Hansberrys and the NAACP win the U.S. Supreme Court case *Hansberry v. Lee;* Carl Hansberry runs for U.S. Congress but is defeated.

**1944**

Lorraine Hansberry graduates from Betsy Ross Elementary School and enters Englewood High School; during her freshman year, she wins a high school writing award for a short story about football.

**1946**

Carl Hansberry dies of cerebral hemorrhage in Mexico, where he had planned to relocate his family to escape U.S. racism.

**1947**

Elected president of high school debating society; attends plays such as Shakespeare's *Othello,* starring Paul Robeson. Jackie Robinson becomes first African American in major league baseball.

**1948**

Graduates from Englewood High School; enters University of Wisconsin at Madison and studies art, literature, stage design, and geology; sees Irish play *Juno and the Paycock.*

**1949**

Studies art at the University of Guadalajara program in Aji-jic, Mexico.

**1950**

Drops out of the University of Wisconsin; studies art in Chicago at Roosevelt University; moves to New York City and takes courses in photography, fiction writing, and jewelry making.

**1951**

Gets involved in radical black politics; becomes youngest staff member on Paul Robeson's publication *Freedom*. *Catcher in the Rye* by J.D. Salinger is published.

**1952**

Meets Robert Nemiroff on picket line protesting segregated sports at New York University; gives a speech in Uruguay for Paul Robeson and has passport revoked; becomes associate editor of *Freedom*.

**1953**

Marries Nemiroff and settles in Greenwich Village; studies African history and culture under W.E.B. Du Bois at Jefferson School of Social Science; resigns from *Freedom* to pursue playwriting.

**1953–1956**

Works menial day jobs while writing three plays.

**1954**

U.S. Supreme Court finds segregated schools unconstitutional in *Brown v. Board of Education*.

**1955**

Rosa Parks is arrested in Montgomery, Alabama, for refusing to give up her seat on a bus to a white passenger, sparking a bus boycott.

**1956**

Nemiroff's pop song "Cindy, Oh, Cindy" becomes a hit, enabling Hansberry to write full time. U.S. Supreme Court outlaws segregated buses in Montgomery.

**1957**

Finishes *A Raisin in the Sun* and enters into collaboration with producer Philip Rose to fund and produce the play. The school desegregation crisis occurs in Little Rock, Arkansas, involving Governor Orval Faubus. *On the Road* by Jack Kerouac is published.

### 1959

*Raisin,* starring Sidney Poitier, opens on Broadway; it wins the New York Drama Critics' Circle Award.

### 1960

Writes two screenplays of *Raisin,* both of which are rejected by Columbia Pictures; her third, least controversial screenplay is accepted; writes slavery drama *The Drinking Gourd* for NBC, but it is never produced because it is considered too controversial; begins work on *The Sign in Jenny Reed's Window* and *Les Blancs.* Lunch counter sit-ins begin in North Carolina; Student Nonviolent Coordinating Committee (SNCC) is founded.

### 1961

Film of *Raisin* is released; wins Cannes Film Festival Award. Freedom Riders force integration of buses in Alabama.

### 1962

Writes *What Use Are Flowers?;* moves to Croton-on-Hudson, New York. The University of Mississippi is integrated by James Meredith, with the backing of the federal government. *One Flew Over the Cuckoo's Nest* by Ken Kesey and *Catch-22* by Joseph Heller are published.

### 1963

Becomes involved in civil rights movement and SNCC; confronts Attorney General Robert Kennedy regarding administration's efforts against racism; scene from *Les Blancs,* Hansberry's new play about European colonialism in Africa, is staged in New York; is diagnosed with cancer and undergoes surgery.

The school desegregation crisis occurs in Alabama when Governor George Wallace attempts to resist integration; Martin Luther King Jr. gives his "I Have a Dream" speech; *The Feminine Mystique* by Betty Friedan is published.

### 1964

Obtains divorce but continues collaboration with Nemiroff; writes text for SNCC's *The Movement: Documentary of a Struggle for Equality;* gives "Young, Gifted, and Black" speech to United Negro College Fund writing contest winners; her new play, *The Sign in Sidney Brustein's Window,* opens on Broadway to mixed reviews and gets support from actors and fans who make it a cause.

Civil rights workers are killed in Mississippi; Martin Luther King Jr. wins the Nobel Peace Prize; gender discrimination is outlawed in federal civil rights legislation.

**1965**

Hansberry dies on January 12, the same day that *The Sign in Sidney Brustein's Window* closes. Malcolm X is assassinated; race riots in Watts, Los Angeles, break out.

**1966**

SNCC adopts black power philosophy; National Organization for Women (NOW) is formed.

**1967**

The two-year anniversary of Hansberry's death is celebrated with a seven-hour radio documentary (*Lorraine Hansberry in Her Own Words),* produced by Nemiroff with recorded performances by sixty-one of America's greatest actors.

**1968**

Martin Luther King Jr. is assassinated.

**1969**

*To Be Young, Gifted, and Black*—a play by Nemiroff assembled from Hansberry's autobiographical writings—opens in New York off-Broadway, runs for 380 performances, and is published as a book.

**1970**

*Les Blancs* (completed by Nemiroff) opens on Broadway to mixed reviews and runs for 40 performances.

**1970–1972**

National tour of *Young, Gifted, and Black.*

**1972**

*The Drinking Gourd* and *What Use Are Flowers?* is published with *Les Blancs* (*The Collected Last Plays of Lorraine Hansberry,* edited by Nemiroff); *To Be Young, Gifted, and Black* is made into a film for educational TV; the revival of *Sidney Brustein* (produced by Nemiroff, adapted by Nemiroff and Charlotte Zaltzberg). Gloria Steinem founds *Ms.* magazine; Equal Rights Amendment passes U.S. Congress.

## 1973

*Raisin* (musical adaptation produced and written by Nemiroff and Zaltzberg) opens on Broadway, wins Tony Award as best musical of 1973–1974, and runs for 874 performances. Abortion rights are established by U.S. Supreme Court (*Roe v. Wade*).

## 1986

*Toussaint* excerpt is published; as the "Twenty-Fifth Anniversary Revival," *Raisin* (directed by Harold Scott) is revived at Roundabout Theatre in New York; Amiri Baraka publishes tribute to Hansberry in *Washington Post*.

## 1989

*A Raisin in the Sun* (Roundabout Theatre production, now starring Danny Glover and Esther Rolle) is directed by Bill Duke for American Playhouse/PBS television.

## 1991

Robert Nemiroff dies on July 18.

## 1992

*A Raisin in the Sun, the Unfilmed Original Screenplay*, edited by Robert Nemiroff, is published.

## 1994

*What Use Are Flowers?* is produced in Atlanta.

# FOR FURTHER RESEARCH

## PLAYS

*Lorraine Hansberry: The Collected Last Plays (Les Blancs, The Drinking Gourd, What Use Are Flowers?).* Ed. Robert Nemiroff, New York: New American Library, 1983.

*A Raisin in the Sun.* New York: Signet, 1988.

A Raisin in the Sun: *The Unfilmed Original Screenplay.* Ed. Robert Nemiroff. New York: Plume/Penguin, 1992.

*The Sign in Sidney Brustein's Window.* New York: Random House, 1965.

## NONFICTION

"An Author's Reflections: Willy Loman, Walter Younger, and He Who Must Live," *Village Voice,* August 12, 1959.

"The Legacy of W.E.B. Du Bois," *Freedomways,* Winter 1965.

*The Movement: Documentary of a Struggle for Equality.* New York: Simon and Schuster, 1964.

"Negro Writer and His Roots: Toward a New Romanticism," *Black Scholar,* March/April 1981.

"On Arthur Miller, Marilyn Monroe, and 'Guilt,'" *Women in Theatre: Compassion and Hope.* Ed. Karen Malpede. New York: Drama Book, 1983. Also contains "On Strindberg and Sexism."

"Original Prospectus for the John Brown Memorial Theatre of Harlem," *Black Scholar,* July/August, 1979.

"The Scars of the Ghetto," *Monthly Review,* February 1965.

"The Shakespearean Experience," *Show,* February 1964.

## AUDIO RECORDINGS

*Lorraine Hansberry in Her Own Words.* Los Angeles: Pacifica Tape Library, BB4497.01 and BB5348.02.

*Lorraine Hansberry on Her Art and the Black Experience* and *Lorraine Hansberry Speaks Out: Art and the Black Revolution.* New York: Caedmon Records, TC 1352, 1972.

*A Raisin in the Sun.* New York: Caedmon Records, TRS 355, 1972 (original cast).

## VIDEO RECORDINGS

*A Raisin in the Sun.* Directed by Daniel Petrie, Columbia Pictures (128 minutes), 1961. Film, available on videocassette.

*A Raisin in the Sun.* Directed by Bill Duke, PBS American Playhouse (171 minutes), 1989. Television production, available on videocassette.

## ABOUT LORRAINE HANSBERRY AND HER WORKS

James Baldwin, "Lorraine Hansberry at the Summit," *Freedomways*, 1979.

———, "Sweet Lorraine," *Esquire*, November 1969.

C.W.E. Bigsby, *Modern American Drama, 1945–1990.* London: Cambridge University Press, 1991.

Jean Carey Bond, ed., "Lorraine Hansberry: Art of Thunder, Vision of Light," *Freedomways*, 1979.

Steven R. Carter, *Hansberry's Drama: Commitment amid Complexity.* Urbana: University of Illinois Press, 1991.

Anne Cheney, *Lorraine Hansberry.* Boston: Twayne, 1984.

Ossie Davis, "The Significance of Lorraine Hansberry," *Freedomways*, 1965.

Lonne Elder III, "Lorraine Hansberry: Social Consciousness and the Will," *Freedomways*, 1979.

Nat Hentoff, "They Fought—They Fought," *New York Times*, May 25, 1969.

Harold R. Isaacs, "Five Writers and Their African Ancestors: Part II," *Phylon*, 1960.

Woodie King Jr., *Black Theatre: The Making of a Movement.* New York: Insight Media, Video #AQ489, 1978.

Richard M. Leeson, *Lorraine Hansberry: A Resource and Production Sourcebook.* Westport, CT: Greenwood, 1997.

Julius Lester, "*Young, Gifted, and Black: The Politics of Caring,*" *Village Voice*, May 1970.

Robert Nemiroff, "From These Roots: Lorraine Hansberry and the South," *Southern Exposure*, September/October 1984.

*New Yorker*, "The Talk of the Town," May 9, 1959.

Ralph J. Tangney, *The Black Experience in the Creation of Drama.* Princeton, NJ: Films for the Humanities FF–128, 1976 (film).

*To Be Young, Gifted, and Black.* Insight Media: New York, 1969 (video).

*To Be Young, Gifted, and Black: Lorraine Hansberry In her Own Words.* Adapted by Robert Nemiroff. Englewood Cliffs, NJ: Prentice-Hall, 1969.

Margaret B. Wilkerson, "The Sighted Eyes and the Feeling Heart of Lorraine Hansberry," *Black American Literature Forum*, Spring 1983.

## ABOUT *A RAISIN IN THE SUN*

Amiri Baraka, "*A Raisin in the Sun*'s Enduring Passion," in *A Raisin in the Sun (Expanded Twenty-Fifth Anniversary Edition) and The Sign in Sidney Brustein's Window*. Ed. Robert Nemiroff. New York: Plume, 1987.

Lloyd Brown, "Lorraine Hansberry as Ironist: A Reappraisal of *A Raisin in the Sun*," *Journal of Black Studies*, March 1974.

Arthur France, "*A Raisin* Revisited: A Re-evaluation of *A Raisin in the Sun* as a Tragedy," *Freedomways*, Summer 1965.

bell hooks, "*Raisin* in a New Light," *Christianity in Crisis*, February 1989.

Harold R. Isaacs, *The New World of Negro Americans*. New York: John Day, 1963.

Sandra Seaton, "*A Raisin in the Sun*: A Study in Afro-American Culture," *Midwestern Miscellany*, 1992.

Thelma Shinn, "Living the Answer: The Emergence of African American Feminist Drama," *Studies in the Humanities*, December 1990.

Charles J. Washington, "*A Raisin in the Sun* Revisited," *Black American Literature Forum*, Spring 1988.

Margaret B. Wilkerson, "*A Raisin in the Sun:* Anniversary of an American Classic," *Theatre Journal*, December 1986.

# INDEX